DAVID RORIE
POEMS AND PROSE

For the Enlightenment
of my good friend
Ronnie —

Jon

5-8-86

David Rorie was cultured certainly, urbane, suave, whimsical—as one would expect from his writings—with both wit and humour: a perfect combination. The qualities of head and hand and heart of David Rorie are gloriously and abundantly present in his verse and his prose. His songs have gone round the world, wherever men of Scottish blood and sympathies have made their homes. He has been much loved.

Dr Danny Gordon

DAVID RORIE
POEMS AND PROSE

edited with an introduction by
WILLIAM DONALDSON

foreword by
JAMES A D MICHIE

ABERDEEN UNIVERSITY PRESS

First published 1983
Aberdeen University Press
A member of the Pergamon Group

© The David Rorie Society 1983

The publishers gratefully acknowledge
the financial assistance of
the Scottish Arts Council
in the publication of this book

British Library Cataloguing in Publication Data

Rorie, David
  David Rorie poems and prose
  1. English literature—20th century
  I. Title   II. Donaldson, William
  828′.91209   PR6035.01

  ISBN 0-08-030357-9
  ISBN 0-08-030358-7 Pbk

PRINTED IN GREAT BRITAIN
THE UNIVERSITY PRESS
ABERDEEN

Foreword

Dr David Rorie was a well loved, kenspeckle family doctor in such diverse and contrasting places as industrial Lancashire, the Kingdom of Fife and rural Aberdeenshire.

In the course of his duties both as a medical practitioner and as a military man of considerable distinction he came to understand the human condition in all its joys and its sorrows, its frailties and its strength. He possessed the gift of tongues and was able to convey through the craft of poetry the spirit of the ordinary people with whom he came into contact. As he recorded their enjoyment and endurance of life, their optimism and stoical acceptance of fate he plucked upon the very strings of humanity at large.

It was felt by some that David Rorie's contribution had not been sufficiently recognised nor had the works of many of his peers been made available to the wider public they deserved. It was out of this contention that the David Rorie Society sprang. With its formation in 1982 it took as its main object the support and promotion of local literature, song and music whether of Scotland, of the North East or of particular localities. It also undertook to foster interest in the vernacular among young and old through publication of worthwhile poetry and prose which had hitherto been somehow sadly neglected.

The publication, *David Rorie Poems and Prose*, is the Society's first essay to put principle into practice. The Society have entered into happy collaboration with Aberdeen University Press and are hopeful that this publication will be the precursor of many other works which will do their authors justice and honour and afford their readers pleasure and contentment.

James A D Michie
President
The David Rorie Society

Contents

Poems

Prose

Acknowledgements

I would like on behalf of the Society to return thanks to Mrs Alice Mitchell for so kindly making available her father's papers; I should also like to thank her legal adviser Mr Richard Ellis, OBE. I acknowledge with warm gratitude the financial support of The Aberdeenshire Educational Trust, The Charles Murray Memorial Trust, The Aberdeen Medico-Chirurgical Society, and The Bailies of Bennachie. Without the active encouragement of these bodies this book could not have been published. I must acknowledge a debt also to Dr George Philp and Mr Allan Ramsay of *Scotsoun* who provided technical facilities for the recently issued cassette of poems and songs by David Rorie, and to Aberdeen University Alumnus Association for assistance with publicity. A number of individual members of the Society have also made a most valuable contribution: Dr Danny Gordon, friend and junior colleague of David Rorie; Mr James Michie, President of the Society and Director of Education for Grampian Region; Mr Charles King, Convener of the Committee, and Adviser of English, Grampian Regional Council; Miss May Thomson of Cults, formerly Local Librarian, Aberdeen Public Library; Dr Cuthbert Graham, formerly of Aberdeen Journals; and Mr Colin MacLean, Publishing Director of Aberdeen University Press. Particular thanks are also due to Mr R D Kernohan, Editor of *Life and Work*, for his assistance with enquiries, and to Mrs Hilda Patience who typed the manuscript. I should like to express my personal indebtedness to our Society's Secretary and Treasurer, Dr Ian Olson, for his generous support, and his wise counsel on many matters concerning medicine and the medical profession. Finally, I should like to thank members of Dr Rorie's family and those of the general public who responded so readily to my requests for information.

WD

Textual Note

The text used in this edition is that of David Rorie's collected poems, *The Lum Hat Wantin' The Croon and Other Poems* (Edinburgh & London, 1935) with the following changes. I have reversed the order of sections within that volume, so that the earlier poems published in 1920 as *The Auld Doctor* come first, and a broadly chronological arrangement is preserved. I have added one later poem "The Bonnie Lass o' Maggieknockater" from Alexander Keith, ed., *Songs of the North-East* (Aberdeen, 1940). I have restored the epigraph from *The Auld Doctor*, and incorporated most of the 1935 authorial preface as a note to "The Lum Hat Wantin' the Croon". The remainder of the notes are Rorie's own. Authorial head notes have been preserved with the addition of identifying initials. The original glossary has been retained with a number of additions to bring it into accordance with modern usage.

The prose content of the present volume has been collected for the first time. I have condensed to suit my purpose, and indicated elisions in the normal fashion. Unless otherwise stated, all extracts were originally published in *The Caledonian Medical Journal*. As this is intended to be a popular edition, I have dispensed with detailed source references.

David Rorie's manuscripts are deposited within Aberdeen Public Library.

WD

Introduction

David Rorie was born in Edinburgh in 1867 where his father, George Livingston Rorie, was a manager with the Royal Bank of Scotland. He received his early education at the Collegiate School of Aberdeen, and was then enrolled in the Medical Faculty at the University of Edinburgh where he graduated in 1890. He practised at Barrow-in-Furness in Lancashire and then at Old Deer in Aberdeenshire before settling in 1894 at Cardenden near Auchterderran, a mining town in Fife a few miles from Kirkcaldy.

Following the great revival of interest in popular antiquities in the closing decades of the nineteenth century, the science of Folklore was founded, and much field-research was going on both in Scotland and England. Although the Forth and Tay bridges had made Fife more accessible, there remained a strong sense of regional identity, of separation and difference from the rest of Scotland, a social conservatism that intrigued the young city-bred physician. Rorie was for a time Medical Officer at Bowhill Colliery, and his work brought him into daily contact with tradition-bearers among the miners and fishermen on the southern shores of the Kingdom. He began to collect the traditional customs and beliefs that had survived amongst them, and later published an essay in the *County Folk-Lore* series, based on his research (in John Ewart Simkins, *Examples of Printed Folk-Lore concerning Fife*, Folk-Lore Society, 1914).

His first love, however, was the folklore of medicine, that body of orally-transmitted beliefs relating to pathology and physiology, hygiene and health, diseases and remedies, obstetrics, gynaecology, and *materia medica*. In 1901, he was elected to the Caledonian Medical Society and later became its President and joint-editor of its *Journal*. The Society had been founded by Highland medical students at the University of Edinburgh during the 1870s to promote the study of Celtic folk-medicine preserved in ancient manuscripts, and to survey contemporary beliefs and practices in the Gaelic-speaking Highlands. Rorie was not, so far as I am aware, a Gaelic speaker, but his own studies in Fife and Aberdeenshire must clearly be seen in this setting. Many of his poems spring directly from it. One thinks of 'Elspet', 'The Healin' Herb' or 'The Bane-setter' — which deals with a type of folk-mediciner by no means defunct in Rorie's day.

But his interest in people was never merely academic. His writing developed quite early that characteristic blend of humorous involvement with individual men and women along with a detached, sardonic view of medicine as part of a wider human comedy in which he himself had an active, and not always dignified, role. His notebooks are full of the physical discomforts and inconveniences of doctoring in country districts: the incessant travelling, the constant liability to interruption often in the middle of the night, the endless waiting at confinements, the clamorous obtuseness of patients, the exasperating inroads of quacks, horse-doctors, and prescribing Ministers. The title poem of his first collection, *The Auld Doctor* (London 1920), was originally '*Vita Medici Vita Canis*' ('The life of a physician is the life of a dog'), and it is a recurring theme.

He had an unerring ear for the rich idiomatic Scots that he heard around him, and he began to record characteristic expressions, anecdotes, and popular sayings, and to work these up into finished short stories. A series of them was published in the *Peoples' Friend* (1895–7). They owe, perhaps, a little too much to the manner made fashionable by Ford's *Humorous Scotch Stories*, but even so, they retain a certain vigour. Here, for example, is a passage from 'A Teeth' in which a long-suffering physician is awakened at three o'clock on a winter morning by a patient wanting a tooth extracted:

"Noo be canny wi's doctor, like a man. A teeth's a rale sair thing. Deed, they're no worth a' the fash they are tae ye. I've heard ma mither say I was near deid *gettin* mines, an't strikes me I'll be nearer deid *lossin'* them. But ye're shiverin' wi' cauld, doctor. Awa' an' pit on mair claes, man. I widna like the fowk to say ye got ony ill frae me, an' I'll juist sit here and wark it a wee bit mair lowser or ye're ready."

"You *are* a cowardly fellow James! It's not loose a bit. It's the pulp of your fingers you feel moving—"

"Aweel, aweel. Come on then. Man thae's awesome lookin' nippers ye hae. Haud on or I get a grup o' the back o' the chair. Od! ye hard-herted wratch, ye wadna pit them into a man's mooth *cauld*? Gie them a bit heat ower the lamp, doctor. No ower lang though or ye'll be burnin' ma gums an' they're tender eneugh in a' conscience wi'oot that—"

"None of your nonsense, James; let me see it and have done with it. Do you think I'm to stand here all night waiting on you and your humbug?"

"Hearken till him! Onybody tae hear ye wid think you was the sufferer an' no' me! But a'body kens doctors is a cruel set. Noo see ye tak the richt ane, doctor. Auld Dr. Hasher—but he wis deid lang afore *your* time—he pu'ed ane o' the soondest teeth in ma heid. He said it wis a *mowler*; I ken it wis a *howler*! But ye see he took a guid dram. That's the warst o' you chaps that's exposed to a' weathers an' hae untimeous hoors—"

"Now this is your last chance, James Lyon. Hold your tongue and open your mouth."

"Haud ma tongue? I'll keep ma tongue oot o' yer road wi'oot haudin it. It's an upper teeth, no' a lower ane. I kent fine ye wisna lookin at the richt ane. Shut ma mooth? Ye hae a funny wey o' drawin teeth gin ye dae't wi' the mooth shut or else ye're no ower-ceevil to a sufferin' fellow—AW—YAW—AW-W-W!"

I have got my chance and taken James unawares; the tooth is on the floor and its owner is rocking back and forwards with his head in his hands.

"Is't oot? Eh man doctor, that was a monster. I thocht ma harns was comin' oot wi' the fangs! Gie't in ma hauns or I tak it hame tae Tib! She'll be mair gled nor me—Dinna shout that wey or I'll wauken the bairns? Ye canna blame me because ye hae a hoosefu' o' bairns, doctor. Weel, weel, I'll awa' hame. Ye'll no hae a moothfu' o' speerits tae keep the cauld aff ma stamack—Eh, ye're a Christian an' that's the rale stuff! Noo what's ye're chairge? *Hauf-a-croon!* Ye're no feared! Ye canna chairge for the dram ye ken seein' it's efter hoors an' ye hinna a leecence! I wis only speirin' ony wey for there's deil a bawbee in ma pooch. Gude nicht t'ye, doctor, gude nicht. I'm rale gled I fund ye in."

In 1905 Rorie acquired an extensive practice in Cults on lower Deeside, where he was to work for the remainder of his professional life. In 1908 he was awarded the degree of MD by the University of Edinburgh for a thesis on medical folklore, and he continued to publish articles upon this and related subjects, mainly in the *Caledonian Medical Journal*. The *Journal* relied upon members of the Society for contributions and it had a strongly literary and antiquarian flavour. For almost thirty years he ran a column in it called 'At the Sign of the Blue Pill' which contains, I think, some of the best of his prose writing. It was an extension of its creator's personality into print, a miscellany of medical matters, poems and songs, reminiscences and whimsies, reflections on politics and the contemporary scene; and as the years went on he became more and more himself. His prose became increasingly refined and he achieved that effortless geniality that marks his non-poetical writing at its best. Rorie's gifts as a public speaker are well-known. One wonders, however, how many of his listeners knew that there existed a body of writing that reflected and extended this skill, and at its best challenged comparison with much of his poetry? I have been able to include a short selection from the 'Blue Pill' in this volume, and the reader may judge for himself.

Rorie had always been attracted by military medicine. He had held a Reserve Commission in his Fife days, and he transferred when he came to Aberdeenshire to a Field Ambulance attached to the 51st (Highland) Division. When the Great War broke out he was mobilised with his unit, although then forty-seven, and embarked for France. It is difficult not to feel that he discovered his true *métier* there; certainly he seems to have regarded it afterwards as the most significant period of his life. In France he found scope for his organisational skill and command of detail; he was resourceful and clear-headed and he won rapid promotion, ending the war as Assistant Director Medical Services to the 51st, a brevet-Colonel with a DSO, Legion of Honour, and two Mentions in Despatches. So he had, then, a 'successful' war; yet he was a civilised man, and he viewed with horror the devastation in Flanders and Northern France. The Field Ambulances often provided medical services for the areas in which they served and his admiration for France—he was a long-standing member of the Franco-Scottish Society—grew into deep affection as a result of regular contact with the civilian population:

At Cramant, I came across an old man while strolling up a steep side road amongst the vines, and with him I got into conversation. It was not altogether easy, as he was practically edentulous, spoke very rapidly, and had a Clemenceau type of moustache covering all his mouth and half his chin. But in spite of these preliminary difficulties we discussed for half an hour—to our mutual edification—the best manures for vines, the main differences between Catholic and Protestant worship, the connection (or want of it) between Church and State in France, and what was best for his chronic indigestion. At this stage I got rather a shock, for he said suddenly, "Pardon, monsieur! Mais vous, vous êtes Italien, n'est-ce-pas?" And when I had explained to him, that in spite of all temptation to belong to that estimable allied nation, I still remained a Scotsman, he started off at

once on Marie Stuart and her history. Then he stopped and shook his head:—
"For the Scots, yes—you are our ancient allies! But the English! Ah, the English!"
I asked him what the trouble was, and he said sadly: "Of course, they too are our
allies and we must love them; but for me it is difficult!" And the difficulty on
further enquiry turned out to be—*Jeanne D'Arc*! He gave me a learned and
emotional *résumé* of her treatment, receiving my respectful sympathy; and I left
him in the middle of the dusty cart-track, bowing, with his battered straw hat in
hand, a farewell; while he tearfully murmured, "Qui! C'est difficile! La pauvre
Pucelle!" For out of the ancient dust, watered with tears, of such memories and
prejudices, national sentiment is, century by century, moulded and remoulded.

[*A Medico's Luck in the War*, Aberdeen 1929]

He maintained his interest in military affairs after the War, retaining his
rank, and serving as Honorary Colonel of RAMC units 51st (Highland)
Division. He was also one of the founders of the Aberdeen branch of the
Royal British Legion, and was its President for more than twenty years.

In 1920 he brought out his first collection of poems, *The Auld Doctor*. He
was encouraged to take this step by the warm advocacy and support of Dr
Charles Murray, the author of *Hamewith*, and the leading literary figure in
Northeast Scotland of his day. They had become friends before the War,
and continued to meet whenever Murray came home on leave from South
Africa. It is obvious from the correspondence that Rorie was anxious about
introducing his verses to a wider public, fearing that they were too medical
and too 'strong' for a general readership. Murray wrote:

> I wish I could have had a talk with you over the publishing. I don't see how you
> can cut out lines as that would emasculate it to a deplorable extent. Still I wonder
> what would the general reader say or think and would booksellers object to its
> being on their counters. I don't know what the attitude of the godly Scot is,
> perhaps he has changed since my day. *You* will know. I feel if it were found
> necessary to cut out lines to get it published in the ordinary way I would rather see
> it published privately or by subscription or some way by which your admirers and
> all who can appreciate humour and human nature can get copies. . . . I wish I could
> spend an evening on them with you just finding as much fault as I could, as I used
> to do to a friend who published a Horace and as he did to me to both our
> advantage. Not mind you that I see anything to find fault with but I would *try* to
> find things just to be sure you had really done your best.   [7 January 1920]

Murray went on to recommend Rorie to his own publisher, Constable, and
to advise him on the best outlet for his verses amongst the London
periodicals. Rorie decided to print the poems as they stood, and when the
volume was published in the winter of 1920, it was enthusiastically received.
Neil Munro wrote:

> I have so hugely enjoyed your "Auld Doctor" that I feel compelled to write you
> saying so, though the chucking of bouquets at authors personally unknown to me
> is no habit of mine. I have chuckled over every line of it.
>
> For years I have known "The Lum Hat Wantin' The Croon" and "The Pawky
> Duke" . . . and some unknown benefactor several years ago sent me a printed copy
> of "Tam and the Leeches", but I never suspected what good stuff you were shyly
> hiding away in the medical journals.

This, sir, is an Occasion! I feel like taking out my bagpipes (they really exist, though I haven't touched them for twenty years), and playing a "Salute to the Bard".

Please keep it up! [28 November 1920]

During the 'twenties and 'thirties his reputation grew. He was a member of two quaintly-named Northeast societies, the 'Calm Soughers' and the 'Sit Siccars', and at their convivial meetings he met congenial spirits like Charles Murray, J F Tocher, and Alexander Keith. He was a leading light in the Aberdeen Medico-Chirurgical Society and frequently enlivened its annual dinners with verses composed for the occasion, the best of which, 'The Tribe o' Galen', is reprinted here. He broadcast regularly from Aberdeen to a wide and appreciative radio audience. Yet his professional commitments remained heavy. He had been Chairman of the Aberdeenshire Panel Committee since 1912, and at various times served also as President of the Aberdeen Branch of the British Medical Association and Chairman of the Division. He was forced to retire from general practice owing to serious illness in 1933, and in 1935 he brought out his collected poems under the title *The Lum Hat Wantin' The Croon and Other Poems* (Edinburgh and London) which forms the basis of the present edition. During the Second World War he chaired the Aberdeen Medical Board of the Ministry of Labour and National Service. He died on 18 February 1946.

David Rorie was an occasional poet, whose reputation during much of his life rested on a handful of poems like 'The Lum Hat' and 'The Pawky Duke' which found their way into widely accessible sources. Most of his published work was scattered in private professional publications, and small-circulation anthologies and periodicals, or else existed only in manuscript form for the appreciation of a discriminating circle of friends. 'The Lum Hat Wantin' The Croon' was written while he was working in Barrow-in-Furness in the 1890s. He came to maturity early as a poet, and these verses at once establish what is usually thought of as the 'Rorie manner': the mordant wit, the verbal assurance, the audacious rhyming, the extravagant, surreal logic; the result is a high-quality Victorian whimsy which would not suffer by comparison with Edward Lear, Lewis Carroll, or W S Gilbert. Yet it comes from a different world because it draws its strength from a different tradition, the centuries of Scottish popular ballads and song in which its creator was deeply versed:

> The burn was big wi' spate,
> An' there cam' tum'lin' doon
> Tapsalteerie the half o' a gate,
> Wi' an auld fish-hake an' a great muckle skate,
> An' a lum hat wantin' the croon.

> The auld wife stude on the bank
> As they gaed swirlin' roun',
> She took a gude look an' syne says she:
> "There's food an' there's firin' gaun to the sea,
> An' a lum hat wantin' the croon."

> Sae she gruppit the branch o' a saugh,
> An' she kickit aff ane o' her shoon,
> An' she stuck oot her fit—but it caught in the gate,
> An' awa she went wi' the great muckle skate,
> An' the lum hat wantin' the croon.

'The Pawky Duke' exhibits the same qualities, occasionally with even greater effect. The poem was extensively revised before publication, but the corrections and additions tend only to heighten the sense of inspired improvisation which makes it so memorable. The metre is fine, borrowed from the rhythms of the Strathspey, but set drunkenly ajee by the careful placing of the 'Scotch Snap' in some of the right, and many of the wrong, places. It is a study in the grotesque which for all its slightness conjures up images of Dunbar, Urquhart, and Hogg. It is typical Rorie, steeped in tradition, and yet unmistakably his own:

> He dwalt far up a Heelant glen
> Where the foamin' flood an' the crag is,
> He dined each day on the usquebae
> An' he washed it doon wi' haggis.
> Hech mon! The pawky duke!
> Hoot ay! An' a haggis!
> For that's the way that the Heelanters dae
> Whaur the foamin' flood an' the crag is. . . .
>
> Then aye afore he socht his bed
> He danced the Gillie Callum,
> An' wi's Kilmarnock owre his neb
> What evil could befall him?
> Hech mon! The pawky duke!
> What evil could befall him?
> When he cast his buits an' soopled his cuits
> Wi' a gude-gaun Gillie Callum.

In some ways, however, these songs are not typical of Rorie's work although he remained alive to the absurd throughout his career. His main preoccupations are more sombre—the tragic inevitability of age and death, the futility of human aspiration, the hypocrisy and backbiting prevalent in small communities. Perhaps this is a reflection of his personality; but there is a professional aspect involved as well. Except in such areas as trauma and childbirth, the Edwardian physician had little to offer the patient except himself. There was virtually nothing in the way of specific or effective therapies, and if one was sensitive, medicine could be a very frustrating and grim career at this time. The outlook is also strongly present in the most important single source for his verses, the popular proverbs and quasi-proverbial lore he recorded from his patients and carefully stored in his notebooks. Some of his poems, like 'The Sibyl', 'The Cynic', 'Isie', and 'Here Aboots', are merely expanded popular aphorisms and these are often the least successful. The original verbal formulae are sometimes quite intense and striking, but their wisdom tends to be conventional and not even

xvi

Rorie can invest them with originality. He is at his best when he generalises the assumptions implicit in popular lore and clothes them in words of his own. One thinks here of the communal pessimism which inspires a poem like 'Tinkler Pate'.

It is important to realise how pervasive the theme is. The speaker in 'The Milestane' is going to die behind a dyke and doesn't seem to care; the crow in 'The Pharisee' curses the pigeon and is blown to bits, 'beak an' claw an' feather'; the corpse in 'The Precaution' is laid to rest under a flattering, lying headstone 'it'll cost a bonny puckle siller/An' he's no warth it'; Elspet implores the dark powers to keep her alive and kill other people. One could go on: 'Life's a dish that's sizzont mair wi' bitter nor wi' sweet' ('Trachelt')—'Man's chief end is naethin' but to cut his brither's throat' ('The Deil's a Busy Bishop'). In 'Ilka dog has but his day', life is seen typically to be dogged with ill-success: 'The game was warth the can'le, though?/Ye think it? Whiles I hae my doots'; the young mock the old, death is resistless, there is neither change nor progress in human affairs. The highest virtue is grim endurance: 'Frae the hippen to the shroud. . . . Bairnheid till eild. . . . Haud fast an' dinna yield' ('The Bell').

But Rorie is not really a philosophical poet in the sense that he develops a system of his own; he tends as we have seen to accept the received wisdom of the folk. He is at his best as a witty observer of men and manners, and he early discovered a form which reflected the strengths of such material, namely the short dramatic monologue which one sees in 'The Short Cut', 'The Precaution', 'The News', 'Neebors', 'The Pacifist', 'The Obituary Notice', 'The Picnic', and 'Droggie'. They share a number of features: a vigorous and idiomatic direct speech accommodated within a subtle and varied metre, a light sprinkling of unobtrusive rhyme, and a highly ironical standpoint which enables the speaker not only to expose and, by implication, condemn the community, but also sometimes himself. These poems tend to be highly economical. In 'The Obituary Notice', for example, the public standing acquired by the deceased during years of calculated respectability is demolished by a grunt:

> Ony wey, the cratur's awa
> An' here's a lang bittie aboot 'im i' the papers.
> "Much respeckit member o' the community."
> Imph'm.

Even the most unattractive of Rorie's characters, however, are regarded with a withering affection, and rescued from the contempt of author and reader by virtue of their sheer verbal energy. In one poem, 'Time Was', he takes his usual technique a stage further, and the monologue—that of a Highland preacher on the vanity of women—is framed by contrasting views of the men and women of the congregation after the service. It is dated 1926, the only one of his poems to show this feature, and its quality is strongly reminiscent of the early Hugh MacDiarmid. One wonders if he had been reading *Sangschaw* (published the year before), although there is little trace of such influence elsewhere.

Ultimately, perhaps, we value Rorie's poetry not so much for its content, as for its felicity, its verbal inventiveness, its demotic urgency. Poem after poem suddenly comes alive in moments like this:

> An' noo it kin' o' cam' to me
> 'Twas maybe some unchancy
> To lat a muckle Frenchy see
> Ye kissin' his financy;
> ['Pauline's Poilu']

Or this, when an old wife is having her first photograph taken:

> Neist shot he had at puir auld Meg,
> The cratur crampit i' the leg,
> An' while he's cursin' throw his cloot,
> She bude to rise an' stramp aboot.
> ['The Likeness']

Or this, on the woes of marriage:

> A reekin' lum's ill, but a wife wi' a raird
> Is fit to gar ony man bite on his baird,
> An' ban the bleck day he was iver ta'en in
> By a yatterin' lump o' original sin.
> ['Tak' Tent']

The reader will find similar examples throughout his work.

David Rorie's verse was the occasional recreation of an accomplished natural stylist and it would be wrong to judge it in other terms. What he does well, he does very well indeed, and I think we may assign him a higher place than the 'gangrel's stance' which he wryly claimed for himself 'on the lower slopes of Helicon'.

William Donaldson

Not mine to let the hair grow long, and talk
In raptured accents of the Higher Things,
Of all the purple Polyanthus bears,
And beating wings.

(Oh no! Nothing of that sort!)

Ne'er have I languished on the lower slopes
Of sweet Parnassus in the thrice-dead years,
Chanting in fathoms of the fathomless
To kindred ears.

(Certainly not! No time for it!)

Nor mine the gift—O, gilded gift and grand!
To linger near the murmur of the Nine,
To mouth in music of the meaningless,
Nay! Never mine!

(That's so! Quite!)

But here to han'le the auld crambo-clink
On hame-owre themes weel-kent by Galen's tribe,
Regairdless o' what ither fowk may think
Or ca' the scribe!

(Ay! That's about it noo!)

THE AULD DOCTOR

O' a' the jobs that sweat the sark
Gie me a kintra doctor's wark,
Ye ca' awa frae dawn till dark,
Whate'er the weather be, O!

Some tinkler wife is in the strae,
Your boots is owre the taps wi' clay
Through wadin' bog an' sklimmin' brae
The besom for to see, O!

Ye ken auld Jock o' Windybarns?
The bull had near ca'ed oot his harns,
His een was blinkin' fu' o' starns,
An' doon they ran for me, O!

There's ae guid wife, we're weel acquaint,
Nae trouble's kent but what she's taen't,
Yet aye she finds some new complaint,
O' which I hae the key, O!

She's had some unco queer mishaps,
Wi' nervish wind and clean collapse,
An' naethin' does her guid but draps—
Guid draps o' barley-bree, O!

I wouldna care a docken blade,
Gin her accoont she ever paid,
But while she gi'es me a' her trade,
There's ne'er a word o' fee, O!

Then De'il hae a' thae girnin' wives,
There's ne'er a bairn they hae that thrives,
It's aye the kink-hoast or the hives
That's gaun to gar them dee, O!

Tak' ony job ye like ava!
Tak' trade, the poopit or the law,
But gin ye're wise ye'll haud awa
Frae medical degree, O!

THE CRAMBO-CLINK

Afore there was law to fleg us a',
An' schedule richt frae wrang,
The man o' the cave had got the crave
For the lichtsome lilt o' sang.
Wife an' strife an' the pride o' life,
Woman an' war an' drink;
He sang o' them a' at e'enin's fa'
By aid o' the crambo-clink.

When the sharpest flint made the deepest dint,
An' the strongest worked his will,
He drew his tune frae the burnie's croon
An' the whistlin' win' o' the hill.
At the mou' o's cave to pleesure the lave,
He was singin' afore he could think,
An' the wife in-bye hush'd the bairnie's cry
Wi' a swatch o' the crambo-clink.

Nae creetic was there wi' superior air
For the singer wha daur decry
When they saw the sheen o' the makar's een,
An' his han' on his axe forbye?
But the nicht grew auld an' he never devaul'd
While ane by ane they would slink,
Awa at a rin to their beds o' skin
Frae the soun' o' the crambo-clink.

THE LUM HAT WANTIN'
THE CROON

I wrote this song one fine summer night nearly forty-five years ago in an English manufacturing town, where the mere thought of a Highland burn in spate was as an ice-cold draught in a parched land. For the singing of it a tune had to be composed—if the word can be rightly used by a man who does not know a note of music—and the finished product was duly 'tried out' on some of my fellow-countrymen. Later, it was published. It was sung in Ladysmith during the siege, and amongst Scots troops in the Great War; I have heard of it in convivial journalistic 'howffs' in Fleet Street; in our own Highlands, and on the Indian frontier; in Canada, Australia, New Zealand, the USA and the South Sea Islands. From all these places, and many more, I have had letters to tell me the writers had either sung it or heard it sung.—DR

    The burn was big wi' spate,
    An' there cam' tum'lin' doon
    Tapsalteerie the half o' a gate,
    Wi' an auld fish-hake an' a great muckle skate,
    An' a lum hat wantin' the croon.

    The auld wife stude on the bank
    As they gaed swirlin' roun',
    She took a gude look an' syne says she:
    "There's food an' there's firin' gaun to the sea,
    An' a lum hat wantin' the croon."

    Sae she gruppit the branch o' a saugh,
    An' she kickit aff ane o' her shoon,
    An' she stuck oot her fit—but it caught in the gate,
    An' awa she went wi' the great muckle skate,
    An' the lum hat wantin' the croon.

    She floatit fu' mony a mile,
    Past cottage an' village an' toon,
    She'd an awfu' time astride o' the gate,
    Though it seemed to gree fine wi' the great muckle skate,
    An' the lum hat wantin' the croon.

    A fisher was walkin' the deck,
    By the licht o' his pipe an' the mune,
    When he sees an auld body astride o' a gate,
    Come bobbin' alang in the waves wi' a skate,
    An' a lum hat wantin' the croon.

    "There's a man overboard!" cries he,
    "Ye leear!" says she, "I'll droon!
    A man on a boord? It's a wife on a gate,
    It's auld Mistress Mackintosh here wi' a skate,
    An' a lum hat wantin' the croon."

Was she nippit to death at the Pole?
Has India bakit her broon?
I canna tell that, but whatever her fate,
I'll wager ye'll find it was shared by a skate,
An' a lum hat wantin' the croon.

There's a moral attached to my sang,
On greed ye should aye gie a froon,
When ye think o' the wife that was lost for a gate,
An auld fish-hake an' a great muckle skate,
An' a lum hat wantin' the croon.

THE PAWKY DUKE

It is hoped that all Scottish characteristics known to the Southron are here: pawkiness and pride of race; love of the dram; redness of hair; eldership of, and objection to instrumental music in the Kirk; hatred of the Sassenach; inability to see a joke, etc. An undying portrait is thus put on record of the typical Scot of the day.—DR

There aince was a very pawky duke,
Far kent for his joukery-pawkery,
Wha owned a hoose wi' a gran' outlook,
A gairden an' a rockery.
Hech mon! The pawky duke!
Hoot ay! An' a rockery!
For a bonnet laird wi' a sma' kailyaird
Is naethin' but a mockery.

He dwalt far up a Heelant glen
Where the foamin' flood an' the crag is,
He dined each day on the usquebae
An' he washed it doon wi' haggis.
Hech mon! The pawky duke!
Hoot ay! An' a haggis!
For that's the way that the Heelanters dae
Whaur the foamin' flood an' the crag is.

He wore a sporran an' a dirk,
An' a beard like besom bristles,
He was an elder o' the kirk
And he hated kists o' whistles.
Hech mon! The pawky duke!
An' doon on kists o' whistles!
They're a' reid-heidit fowk up North
Wi' beards like besom bristles.

His hair was reid as ony rose,
His legs was lang an' bony,
He keepit a hoast an' a rubbin'-post
An' a buskit cockernony.
Hech mon! The pawky duke!
An' a buskit cockernony!
Ye ne'er will ken true Heelantmen
Wha'll own they hadna ony.

Syne ilka fowre hoors through the day
He took a muckle jorum,
An' when the gloamin' gaither'd grey
Got fou wi' great decorum.
Hech mon! The pawky duke!
Blin' fou wi' great decorum!
There ne'er were males amang the Gaels
But lo'ed a muckle jorum.

An' if he met a Sassenach,
Attour in Caledonia,
He gart him lilt in a cotton kilt
Till he took an acute pneumonia.
Hech mon! The pawky duke!
An' a Sassenach wi' pneumonia!
He lat him feel that the Land o' the Leal
'S nae far frae Caledonia.

Then aye afore he socht his bed
He danced the Gillie Callum,
An' wi's Kilmarnock* owre his neb
What evil could befall him?
Hech mon! The pawky duke!
What evil could befall him?
When he cast his buits an' soopled his cuits
Wi' a gude-gaun Gillie Callum.

But they brocht a joke, they did indeed,
Ae day for his eedification,
An' they needed to trephine his heid,
Sae he deed o' the operation.
Hech mon! The pawky duke!
Wae's me for the operation!
For weel I wot this typical Scot
Was a michty loss to the nation.

* The old type of nightcap, woollen, and frequently red, which was much in vogue in bygone days.—DR

5

MACFADDEN AND MACFEE

This ballad is of great interest, and, as far as we know, has not hitherto appeared in print. It is certainly not in Child's Collection. It was taken down from the singing of an aged man of one hundred and five years, in Glen Kennaquhair. Internal evidence would tend to show that the incidents recorded in the ballad occurred in the seventeenth century, and that Sir Walter Scott had heard at least one verse of it. The aged singer—now, alas! no more—sang it to the air of *Barbara Allen.*—DR

It was an' aboot the Lammas time,
In sixteen forty-three, sirs,
That there fell oot the awfu' fecht
'Twixt Macfadden an' Macfee, sirs.

Macfadden, wha was gaun to kirk
Upon the morn's morn,
Had washed his kilt an' cleaned his dirk
An' combed his Sabbath sporran.

An' bein' for the time o' year
Remarkably fine weather,
These articles o' dress were laid
To air upon the heather.

Waes me! Macfee, while dandrin' owre
The bonnie braes o' Lorne,
Maun gang an' pit his muckle fit
Upon Macfadden's sporran.

A piece o' carelessness like this
The brichtest heart would sadden,
An' when he saw the caitiff deed
It fair gaed owre Macfadden.

For he was shavin' at the time,
An' when the sicht he saw, sir,
Wi' rage he shook an' nearly took
His neb aff wi' his raazor.

A while he swore and staunched the gore
An' ere Macfee got ae lick,
Macfadden cursed him heid an' heels
In comprehensive Gaelic.

Syne when his breath was a' but gane,
An' when he couldna say more,
He lat a muckle Heelant yell
An' at him wi' his claymore.

What sweeter sound could warrior hear
Unless it was the daddin'
That echoed oot when'er Macfee
Got hame upon Macfadden?

Nae sweeter soond I weel could ween,
Exc' ppin' it micht be, sirs,
The soond that hurtled oot when'er
Macfadden hit Macfee, sirs.

An awfu' fecht it was to see,
A fecht baith fell an' dour, sirs,
For ere the tuilzie weel began
The glen was fu' o' stour, sirs.

An awfu' fecht, again I say't,
An on each auld clay biggin',
The freends o' baith, like hoodie craws,
Was roostin' on the riggin'.

And aye they buckled till't wi' birr;
In combat sair an' grievous,
They glanced like lightnin' up Strathyre
An' thundered doon Ben Nevis.

Wha won the fecht, or whilk ane lost,
Was hid frae mortal e'e, sirs,
Nane saw the fearsome end o' baith
Macfadden an' Macfee, sirs.

But still they say, at break o' day,
Upon the braes o' Lorne,
Ye'll hear the ghaistly rustlin' o'
Macfadden's Sabbath sporran.

TAM AND THE LEECHES

I

FAITH, there's a hantle queer complaints
To cheenge puir sinners into saints,
An' mony divers ways o' deein'
That doctors hae a chance o' seein'.
The Babylonian scartit bricks
To tell his doots o' Death's dark tricks,
The Greek he kentna hoo 'twas farin'
Across the ferry rowed by Charon,
An' readin' doonwards through the ages
The tale's the same in a' their pages,
Eternal grum'lin' at the load
We hae to bear alang Life's road,
Yet, when we're fairly at the bit,
Awfu', maist awfu' sweer to flit,
Praisin' the name o' ony drug
The doctor whispers in oor lug
As guaranteed to cure the evil,
To haud us here an' cheat the Deevil.
For gangrels, croochin' in the strae,
To leave this warld are oft as wae
As the prood laird o' mony an acre,
O' temporal things a keen partaker.

II

Noo a' this leads up to my tale
O' what befell puir Tam MacPhail,
A dacent miner chiel in Fife
Wha led a maist exemplar' life,
An' ne'er abused himsel' wi' liquor,
But took it canny-like an' siccar.
Aye when he cast his wet pit-breeks,
Tam had a gless that warm'd his cheeks;
For, as it trickled owre his craigie,
He held it wardit aff lumbaigy.
It wasna that he liked the dram,
'Twas pure needcessity wi' Tam!
But twa years syne—or was it three?—
Tam thocht that he was gaun to dee,
An' Faith! they've often gar'd me grew
By tellin' what I'll tell to you.

III

The early tatties had come in
When Tammas's besettin' sin,
A love o' a' this warld's gude things
An' a' the pleesures eatin' brings,
Gar'd him hae sic a bad mischeef
It fleggit him ayont belief!
Pay-Saturday it was, I mind,
An' Jean, intendin' to be kind,
Had biled the firstlins o' her yaird
(For naethin' else Tam wud hae sair'd),
Sae when they cam' frae Jean's clean pat,
Altho' they seemed a trifle wat,
Tam in his hunger ate a meal
That wud hae staw'd the big black Deil,
Syne at his cutty had a draw,
Syne gantit wi' wide-open jaw,
An' aince his heid was on the cod,
He sune was in the land o' Nod.

IV

But when the knock had chappit four
Tam had to rise an' get attour,
For in his bed he couldna bide
He'd sic a steer in his inside!
The granes o'm waukent faithfu' Jean.
An' then began a bonny scene!
A parritch poultice first she tries,
Het plates on plates she multiplies,
But ilka time his puddens rum'les
A' owre the place Tam rows an' tum'les,
For men in sic-like situations,
Gude kens hae gey sma' stock o' patience!
Yet fast the pain grows diabolic,
A reg'lar, riving, ragin', colic,
A loupin', gowpin', stoondin' pain
That gars the sweat hail doon like rain.
Whiles Tam gangs dancin' owre the flair,
Whiles cheeky-on intil a chair,
Whiles some sma' comfort he achieves
By brizzin' hard wi' baith his nieves;
In a' his toilsome tack o' life
Ne'er had he kent sic inward strife,
For while he couldna sit, forbye
Like Washington he couldna lie!

V

Noo, at lang last his guts was rackit
Till Tam was bullerin' fair distrackit,
An' sune wi' roar succeedin' roar
He fosh in a' the fowk neist door,
An' ane o' them—auld Girsie Broon—
She ran an' brocht the doctor doon,
Wha hurried in a' oot o' breath,
For Girsie said 'twas life or death!
The doctor oxter'd Tam till's bed,
Fingert his wame an' shook his head;
"We who pursue the healing art,
See youth commence and age depart,
Pills we prescribe and pulses feel,
Your systems know from scalp to heel!
And here? Potato indigestion,
Of that there's not the slightest question,
While, what my great experience teaches
Is most relief is got from leeches."—
"Awa," yells Tam, "fesh hauf-a-dizzen!
O haste ye, ere I loss my rizzon!"
Sae aff gangs wullin' Girsie Broon,
To wauk the druggist wast the toon.

VI

Noo, Droggie had an awfu' stock,
Tobacco, wreetin' paper, rock,
A' kin' o' wersh tongue-twistin' drinks,
A' kin' o' Oriental stinks,
The best cod liver ile emulsions,
Wee poothers that could cure convulsions,
Famed Peter Puffer's soothin' syrup,
An' stuff to gar canaries chirrup.
He'd toothache tinctur's, cures for corns,
Pomades to gar hair grow on horns,
He'd stuff for healin' beelin' lugs,
He'd stuff for suffocatin' bugs,
He'd stuff for feshin' up your denners,
Against your wull an' a' gude menners,
A' kin' o' queer cahoochy goods
To suit the system's varyin' moods,
Wi' navvies' operatin' peels,
Sookers for bairns an' fishin' reels,
In fac'—but losh! I'd better stop,
The mannie kep' a druggist's shop!
An' in his bauchles an' his breeches
Cam' grum'lin' doon to get the leeches

While, nearly scunnert wi' their squirmin',
Aff hirples Girsie wi' the vermin.

VII

An' noo, my billies, draw a veil,
Till mornin's licht, owre Tam Macphail,
Till aince again the doctor cam'
To see what cheenge was wrocht in Tam.
'Twas nine o'clock he stapt in-bye,
Relieved to hear nae waesome cry.
"Well, well, Macphail!" the doctor says,
"My treatment's worthy of all praise!
I left you—why 'twas like a riot!
I see you now, contented, quiet.
Far, very far, our knowledge reaches!
How did you get on with the leeches?"
Tam ne'er replied, but turn'd his back,
Wi' tearfu' een 'twas Jean wha spak,
"Eh, Doctor!—Sic an awfu' cure
I ne'er saw gi'en to rich or puir,
For when we saw the ugsome beasts
It gart the herts rise in our breists!
But Tam, wha tak's your word for law,
Juist swalla'd doon the first pair raw!
Yet try's he micht, an' sair he tried,
He had to hae the last four fried!"
The doctor turn'd him on his heel,
An' though puir Tam looked rale no-weel,
He couldna trust himsel' to speak,
The tears were rinnin' doon his cheek,
An' a' that day was sair forfaughen
Wi' tryin' to haud himsel' frae lauchin'!

VIII

Whate'er wi' Tam ye chance to crack on,
There's ae thing ye maun ne'er gang back on.
Freely he'll talk on politics,
The weather an' its dirty tricks,
On wages an' the price o' coal
Or things conneckit wi' the soul,
On hoo the meenister's a leear
An' medical advice owre dear,
But if the crack warks roond to leeches,
Puir Tam pits doon his pipe an' retches!

The main incident in this tale was told to me over forty years ago by an old practitioner as having occurred in his practice.—DR

THE HOWDIE

'Twas in a wee bit but-an'-ben
She bade when first I kent her,
Doon the side roadie by the kirk
Whaur Andra was precentor.

An' a' the week he keepit thrang
At's wark as village thatcher,
Whiles sairly fashed by women folk,
Wi' "Hurry up an' catch her!"

Nae books e'er ravel't Tibbie's harns,
Nae college lear had reached her,
An' a' she kent aboot her job
Her ain experience teached her.

To this cauld warld in fifty year
She'd fosh near auchteen hunner.
Losh keep's! When a' thing's said an' dune,
The cratur' was a won'er!

A' gate she'd traivelled day an' nicht,
A' kin' o' orra weather
Had seen her trampin' on the road,
Or trailin' through the heather.

But Time had set her pechin' sair,
As on his way he birled;
The body startit failin' fast
An' gettin' auld an' nirled.

An' syne, to weet the bairnie's heid
Owre muckle, whiles, they'd gie her;
But noo she's deid—ay, mony a year—
An' Andra's sleepin' wi' her.

The custom of 'weetin' the bairn's heid' consisted of drinking a glass of raw whisky in honour of the child's safe arrival. Anyone not so doing was held 'to tak' awa the bairn's luck'.—DR

DAYLICHT HAS MONY EEN

O! can'le-licht's baith braw and bricht
At e'en when bars are drawn,
But can'le-licht's a dowie sicht
When dwinin' i' the dawn.
Yet dawn can bring nae wearier day
Than I hae dree'd yestre'en,
An' comin' day may licht my way—
Daylicht has mony een.

Noo, daylicht's fairly creepin' in,
I hear the auld cock craw;
Fu' aft I've banned him for his din,
An' wauk'nin' o' us a'!
But welcome noo's his lichtsome cry
Sin' bed-fast I ha'e been,
It tells anither nicht's gane by—
Daylicht has mony een.

O! bed-fast men are weary men,
Laid by frae a' their wark;
Hoo thocht can kill ye ne'er will ken
Till tholin' 't in the dark.
But ere nicht fa's I'll maybe see
What yet I hinna seen,
A land whaur mirk can never be—
Daylicht has mony een.

THE BANE-SETTER

Oor Jock's gude-mither's second man
At banes was unco skilly;
It cam' by heirskep frae an aunt,
Leeb Tod o' Nether Tillie.
An' when he thocht to sough awa,
He sent for Jock, ay did he,
An' wulled him the bane-doctorin',
Wi' a' the lave o's smiddy.

A braw doon-settin' 'twas for Jock,
An' for a while it paid him,
For wi's great muckle nieves like mells
He pit in banes wi' smeddum.
Ay! mony a bane he snappit in
At elbuck, thee, an' shouther;
Gin ony wouldna gang his gait,
Jock dang them a' to poother.

Noo, smiddy wark's a droothy job,
Sae whiles Jock wat his whustle,
When wi' a horseshoe or a bane
He'd held some unco tussle.
But even though miracklous whiles,
It mattered nane whativer,
For whaur's the body disna ken
A drucken doctor's cliver?

Ae nicht when Jock was gey weel on,
An' warslin' wi' some shoein',
They brocht a bane case intil him
That proved puir Jock's undoin',
A cadger wi' an auld cork leg,
An' fou as Jock or fouer,
Wha swore that o' his lower limb
He'd fairly lost the pooer.

Jock fin's the leg, an' shaks his heid,
Syne tells the man richt solemn,
"Your knee-pan's slippit up your thee
Aside your spinal column;
But gin ye'll tak a seat owre here,
An' lat them haud ye ticht, man,
I'se warrant for a quart o' beer
I'll quickly hae ye richt, man."

Jock yokit noo wi' rale guid wull
To better the condeetion,
While Corkie swore he had his leg
Ca'd a' to crockaneetion.
Jock banned the lamp—"'twas in his een"—
An' deaved wi' Corkie's granin',
Quo' he, "Gin ye'll pit oot the licht
I'll gey sune pit the bane in!"

Oot went the licht, Jock got his grup,
He yarkit an' he ruggit,
He doobled up puir Corkie's leg,
Syne strauchtened it an' tuggit.
An' while that baith the twa o' them
Was sayin' some orra wordies,
Auld Corkie's leg, wi' hauf o's breeks,
Cam' clean aff at the hurdies.

Jock swat wi' fear, an' in the dark
He crep' attour the smiddy,
For, weel-a-wat, he thocht his wark
Would land him on the widdy.
An' wi' the leg he ran till's hoose,
Just half-way doon the clachan,
His cronies oxterin' Corkie oot,
An' nearly deein' o' lauchin'.

But at Jock's door they stude an hour,
An' vainly kicked an' knockit,
Sin' Jock, in a' the fear o' death,
Had got it barred an' lockit.
An' 'twasna till the neist forenune
They fand the leg, weel hidden,
For Jock was oot afore daylicht
An' stuck it in the midden.

This feenished Jock, an' efter han'
He buckled til his ain wark,
For sune a' owre the kintra-side
They kent aboot his bane wark,
An' hoo a law-wer fleggit Jock
At Corkie's instigation,
An' gart him pay a five-pun' note
By way o' compensation.

*Ne sutor ultra crepidam**
Is gude enough for maist o's,
For aye there's wark that's bude to get
The better o' the best o's.
An' just as doctors canna shoe
Or haud a hin' leg stiddy,
Ye needna seek for surgery
Inside a country smiddy.

* Let the cobbler stick to his last.

BRITHERS

'Twas up at the tree near the heid o' the glen
I keppit a tinkler chiel,
The cauld wind whistled his auld duds through,
He was waesomely doon at the heel;
But he made me free o' his company,
For he kent that I wished him weel.

He lookit me fairly 'tween the een,
He cam' o' an auncient clan;
He gae me gude-day in a freendly way,
While he spak me man to man,
Though my gibbles was a' for the human frame
An' his for kettle an' pan.

"Ye're oot i' the warst that the weather can dae,
Ye're free o' the road, like me,
I palmer aboot for kettles to cloot,
Wi' an orra-like weird to dree;
An' oor job's to men' whativer'll men',
Wi' luck to fix oor fee!"

"Brithers baith o' the auld high road—
Yet the Deil hae General Wade
For learnin's the shauchle instead o' the step
Wi' the weary wark o' his spade,
Till the Jew an' the Sassenach lord it noo
Owre the hills whaur the heroes gaed!"

"O, gang ye East," quo' I, "or Wast,
Or whither awa gang ye?
Will ye come to a hoose whaur a gude man bides,
For a tastin' o' barley bree?
Ye can howk i' the kebbuck an' howk again
As lang as there's kebbuck to pree."

"Or seek ye a saxpence to slocken your drooth?
Ye needna be langer in doot;
Ye can hae a bit hurle to help ye on,
An' I'll get ye a pan to cloot.
I'se warrant I'll freely lat ye in,
An' as freely lat ye oot."

A tuft o' the broom was knotted wi' tow,
An' a rag on't fluttered free,*
While he shook his heid owre some ferlies there,
That I'm bathered if I could see,
Though I kent my soul was sib to his
In a queer freemasonry.

"The wife's a mile on the road afore's,
An' the bairnies farther still;
I canna keep tryst wi' doctor folk,
But I'll borrow the price o' a gill,
An' I'll pay ye back when we've finished oor tack
O' a' that's gude an' ill."

He spat on the siller an' pooched it syne,
An' quately winked an e'e;
"The road's a bond that we canna deny,
An' it's linkit you an' me
In the kindly yoke o' the gaun-about folk,
Whauriver they chance to be!"

On the bowl o's cutty he scartit a spunk,
An' he leggit it doon the wind;
Gin his claes would hae fleggit a bubbly-jock,
Guid Lord! he'd an easy mind!
An' oor forbears maybe were near-hand freen's
For a' that I can find.

* The reference is to the signs left by tinkers and 'gangrels' on bushes etc. to indicate to the others what route they had taken.—DR

THE CYNIC

Cauld blew the blast frae East to Wast,
A blast wi' a smirr o' snaw,
An' it took the doctor's guid lum hat
Richt owre the kirk-yaird wa'.
When he sichtit it he dichtit it,
An' he glowred wi' an angry e'e—
For says auld Jock Smairt, wha was passin' wi' his cairt:
"Ye've a gey gude crap," says he.

Cauld blew the blast frae East to Wast,
A blast baith snell an' keen,
An' the washin' o' the clarty wife
Sailed aff the washin' green,
An' it landit on the midden-heid,
Whaur nae washin' ought to be—
An' says auld Jock Smairt, wha was passin' wi' his cairt:
"Weel, hame's ay hame," says he.

Cauld blew the blast frae East to Wast,
An' it gart the deid leaves loup,
An' it set the shoothers heicher yet
O' the gaithrin' at the roup;
An' stour filled the een o' the unctioneer,
Till the cratur' couldna see;
An' says auld Jock Smairt, wha was passin' wi' his cairt:
"Turn aboot's fair play," says he.

Cauld blew the blast frae East to Wast,
An' the rein catched the grey mear's tail,
An' her heels to save her hin'er en'
Gaed lashin' like a flail.
An' the haill apotheck lay in spails,
As the grey mear warsled free;
An' when auld Jock Smairt saw the fashion o' his cairt:
"Wha's seekin' ony spunks?" says he.

THE NICHT THAT THE BAIRNIE CAM' HAME

I was gaun to my supper richt hungert an' tired,
A' day I'd been hard at the pleugh;
The snaw wi' the dark'nin' was fast dingin' on,
An' the win' had a coorse kin' o' sough.
'Twas a cheery-like sicht as the bonny fire-licht
Gar't the winnock play flicker wi' flame;
But my supper was "Aff for the doctor at aince!"
That nicht that the bairnie cam' hame.

Noo, I kent there was somethin' o' that sort to be,
An' I'd had my ain thochts, tae, aboot it;
Sae when my gude-mither had tel't me to flee,
Fegs, it wisna my pairt for to doot it.
Wi' a new pair o' buits that was pinchin' like sin,
In a mile I was hirplin' deid lame;
'Twas the warst nicht o' a' that I ever pit in,
That nicht that the bairnie cam' hame.

I'd a gude seeven mile o' a fecht wi' the snaw,
An' the road was near smoort oot wi' drift;
While the maister at market had got on the ba',
Sae I'd tint my ae chance o' a lift.
When I passed the auld inn as I cam' owre the hill,
Although I was mebbe to blame,
I bude to gang in-bye an' swallow a gill,
That nicht that the bairnie cam' hame.

"Gude be thankit!" says I, at the doctor's front door,
As I pu'd like mischeef at the bell;
But my he'rt gae a dunt at the story that runt
O' a hoose-keeper body'd to tell.
The man wasna in? He was at the big hoose?
A sick dwam cam' richt owre my wame.
Hoo the deevil was I to get haud o' him noo,
That nicht that the bairnie cam' hame?

The doctor was spendin' the nicht at the laird's,
For the leddy, ye see, was expeckin';
A feckless bit cratur, weel-meanin' an' a',
Though she ne'er got ayont the doo's cleckin'.
It's them that should ha'e them that hinna eneugh,
Fegs, lads, it's a damnable shame!
Here's me wi' a dizzen, and aye at the pleugh
Sin' that nicht that the bairnie cam' hame!

What was I to dae? I was at my wits' en',
For Tibbie the howdie was fou,
An' e'en had I got her to traivel the road
What use was she mair than the soo?
I was switin' wi' fear though my fingers was cauld,
An' my taes they was muckle the same;
Man, my feet was that sair I was creepin' twa-fauld
That nicht that the bairnie cam' hame.

Three hoors an' a hauf sin' I startit awa,
An' Deil faurer forrit was I!
Govy-ding! It's nae mows for the heid o' the hoose
When the mistress has yokit to cry!
A set o' mis-chanters like what I'd come through
The strongest o' spirits would tame,
I was ettlin' to greet as I stude in the street
That nicht that the bairnie cam' hame!

But a voice that I kent soondit richt in my lug,
Frae my he'rt it fair lifted a load
As I tells him my story, for wha should he be
But the factor's son hame frae abroad.
"It's a brute of a night, but to doctor's my trade,
If ye'll have me, my laddie, I'm game!"
An' he druve his ain trap seeven mile through the snaw
That nicht that the bairnie cam' hame.

Ay! an' cracked like a pen-gun the hail o' the road
An' though I was prooder than ask,
When he fand I was grewsin' awa at his side
He filled me near fou frae his flask.
Syne when a' thing was owre an' I gruppit his han'
Says the wife, "We maun gie him the name!"*
An' there's aye been a gude word for him i' the hoose
Sin' the nicht that the bairnie cam' hame.

* 'To gie him the name'—i.e. call the child after him—was, properly, considered a compliment.—DR

HUMAN NATUR'

As I gang roon' the kintra-side
Amang the young an' auld,
I marvel at the things I see
An' a' the lees I'm tauld.
There's Mistress—weel, I winna say:
I wadna hurt her pride,—
But speerits hae a guff, gude-wife,
Nae peppermints can hide.

Then there's the carle I said maun bide
In bed or I cam' back,
An' frae the road I saw him fine
Gang dodgin' roond a stack;
I heard him pechin' up the stair
As I cam' in the door—
But Faith! My lad was in his bed
An' ettlin' for to snore.

An' here's a chap that needs a peel,
He chaws it roon' an' roon',
He's narra' i' the swalla', an'
He canna get it doon.
Yet whiles his swalla's wide eneuch,
The muckle ne'er-dae-weel,
Gin it had aye been narra'er
He hadna nott the peel.

Ye tend them a', baith great an' sma',
Frae cradle to the grave,
An' add to sorrows o' your ain
The tribbles o' the lave,
An' yet ye find they're a' the same,
When human natur's watched,
It's no ill deeds they haud as wrang—
The sin o't 's when they're catched.

ANG-BANG-PANG

O hae ye heard the latest news
O' Mistress Mucklewame?
Her doctor hadna pickit up
Her trouble here at hame,
Sae they took her tae a speeshalist
To fin' oot what was wrang,
An' it seems noo a' the bother
Has been ang-bang-pang.

Faith, in the marriage market then
Her man's had little luck,
She's just a muckle creishy lump
That waddles like a juck;
But the nerves gaun through her body's
Been the trouble a' alang,
An' it's complicated noo, ye see,
By ang-bang-pang.

I've aye held oot oor doctor
Was a skeely man afore,
But I'll never lat the cratur noo
A stap inside the door!
A' up an' doon the parish
It has made a bonny sang,
That he didna ken his neebor's wife
Had ang-bang-pang.

They've pit her in hot-water baths
To lat the body steep,
They're feedin' her on taiblets
Frae the puddens o' a sheep,
They're talkin' o' a foreign spaw
Upon the continang,
They think they'll maybe cure her there
O' ang-bang-pang.

There's mony ways o' deein' that
Oor faithers didna ken,
For ae way foond in "Buchan", noo
The doctors gie us ten;
But I hope to a' the Pooers abune
Auld Death may be owre thrang
To come an' smoor my vital spark
Wi' ang-bang-pang.

THE SPEESHALIST

SATURDAY NIGHT

Noo, ye'll no tak' it ill o' me, Mistress Macqueen,
For ye ken ye are juist a young kimmer,
An' I am a mither that's beerit fourteen,
An' forty year mairrit come simmer;
When ye see your bit bairnie there drawin' up her knees,
Wi' grups in her little interior,
Juist gie her a nip o' a gude yalla cheese,
An' ye'll find that there's naethin' superior!

The doctor had said that ye shouldna row'r ticht,
Ye should aye gie the wee cratur's belly scope?
Awa wi' the lang-leggit lum-hattit fricht
Wi' his specks an' his wee widden tellyscope!
What kens he o' littlens? He's nane o' his ain,
If she greets it juist keeps the hoose cheerier,
See! THAT was the wey I did a' my fourteen,
An' ye'll find that there's naethin' superior!

I tell ye, noo, warkin' fowk canna draw breath,
What wi' sanitries, cruelties, an' bobbies,
An' the doctors would pit ye in fair fear o' death
Wi' their blethers o' German macrobbies!
I've been at their lecturs on health an' High Jean,
Gude kens that I niver was wearier!
Use your ain commonsense when ye're treatin' your wean,
An' ye'll find that there's naethin' superior!

SUNDAY MORNING

She's awa'? Weel, ma wumman, I thocht that mysel',
When I saw your blind doon frae oor corner,
An', says I, "I'll juist tak' a step up-bye an' tell
Twa or three things it's better to warn her."
'Twas the doctor's negleck o'r, the auld nosey-wax!
There's naethin' to dae noo, but beery her,
Tammy Chips mak's a kist here at seeven-an'-sax,
An' ye'll find that there's naethin' superior!

ISIE

The wife she was ailin', the doctor was ca'ed,
She was makkin' eneuch din for twa,
While Peter was suppin' his brose at the fire,
No heedin' the cratur' ava.
"Eh, doctor! My back's fair awa wi' it noo,
It was rackit the day spreadin' dung;
Hae, Peter! Come owre wi' the lamp, like a man,
Till the doctor can look at my tongue!"

But Peter had bade wi' her near forty year,
Fine acquaint wi' her weel-soopled jaw,
Sae he lowsed his tap button for ease till his wame,
Wi' a gant at the wag-at-the-wa'.
"Weel, Isie," says he, "an' it's me that should ken,
That's the ae place ye niver hae cramp.
The lamp's bidin' here: if he's seekin' a sicht
O' yer tongue he can trail't to the lamp!"

THE HYPOCHONDRIAC

I dinna ken what is the maitter wi' Jeams,
He canna get sleepit at nicht for his dreams,
An' aye when he waukens he granes and he screams
Till he fair pits the shakers on me!

Can ye no mak' up somethin' to gie him a sleep?
I'm tellin' ye, doctor, he gars my flesh creep,
Till I'm that fu' o' nerves that the verra least cheep
Noo juist fair pits the shakers on me!

Wi' his meat he was aince a man easy to please,
But last Sabbath he flang the fried ingans an' cheese
That I had for his supper richt into the bleeze,
An' he fair pits the shakers on me!

Then he sat in the ingle an' chowed bogie-roll,
An' read "Jowler's Sermons" an' talked o' his soul,
Faith! conduc' o' that sort's no easy to thole,
For it fair pits the shakers on me!

He's plenty o' siller, ye're sure o' your fee,
Just gie him a soondin', an' gin he's to dee,
Come oot wi' the truth—dinna fash for a lee,
It'll no pit the shakers on me!

What! "Juist heepocondry? Nocht wrang wi' his chest?"
The Deil flee awa wi' the man for a pest!
To think o' me lossin' sae mony nichts' rest
An' him pittin' the shakers on me!

Ay, though he may rout like the bull in the park,
I'se warrant the morn he's on wi' his sark,
An' aff wi' the rest o' the men till his wark,
For he'll no pit the shakers on me!

THE AULD CARLE

The auld man had a girnin' wife,
An' she was aye compleenin',
For a' kin' o' orra things
The body aye was greenin'.
It's "I'll try this," and "I'll try that,"
At ilka adverteesement,
She flang his siller richt an' left
An' niver got nae easement.

The carle he led sic a life
The haill thing was a scunner,
Sae ae braw day his birse was up
He fairly roondit on her.
"Ye're aye gaun to dee, gúde-wife—
Fowre nichts I hinna sleepit,
Gin it's to be, I wush to peace
Ye'd set a day an' keep it!"

Wow! noo there was a tirravee!
An angry wife was she, than!
"An' is it no my ain affair
The day I'm gaun to dee, than?
Aha! ye think ye'll tryst the wricht
An' rid him o' his timmer?
Syne haud anither waddin' wi'
Some feckless, thowless limmer!"

Awyte, but noo she's fu' o' life,
She's ta'en anither tack o't!
An' aye that she flees oot on him
His words is at the back o't!
Sae keep your tongue atween your teeth
When ettlin' to be cliver,
Ense ye'll be like the auld carle
An' en' waur aff than iver!

THE FEE

In the heicht o' the foray
Sir Raif got a clour,
Sir Raif the regairdless
In battle sae dour.
O cleanly the saddle
They ca'ed him attour!

Then aid for his wounds
He did sairly beseech,
An' aff to the greenwood
In shade o' a beech
They hurried auld Simon
The kintra-side's leech.

Wi' a tow roon' his neck
Simon knelt on his knee,
An' he saw as he glow'red
Wi' the tail o' his e'e
That armed men held it
Owre bough o' the tree.

"Noo, Simon, to heal
Is your trade, no' to kill,"
Quo' Sir Raif. "An' though, mark ye,
We dootna your skill,
Grup the tow, knaves! If need be
Pull up wi' a will!"

"But what o' my fee,
Noo I ask ye, Sir Raif?"
"Gin I live, Master Simon,
I'll wager it's safe!
There! Laugh not, ye villains,
His neck ye may chafe!"

O stanched was the blue blude
That ran on the grass,
Sae eident was Simon
His skill to surpass,
Sir Raif was in fair way
His foes to harass.

An' the fee they gae Simon—
The tale is aye rife—
For fittin' Sir Raif
To wield sword i' the strife?
'Twas the greatest e'er gi'en—
For they gae him his life!

HERE ABOOTS

Doon in the placie I hae my hame
We're an ill-daein' pack o' deils,
For ilk ane gangs a gait o' his ain
An' the lave play yap at his heels.
It's argy-bargy—awfu' wark!
An' whiles we come to blows
Till a man's ill-natur' lappers his sark
As it sypes awa frae his nose.

The rizzon o't's no' far to seek,
I'll tell ye plump an' plain,
We ken oor neebours' business best—
The Deil may hae oor ain!
The wricht's a billy for settin' banes,
The meenister deals in pills,
The doctor thinks his gift's to preach
An' the pollisman mak's oor wills!

There's whiles I think we're waur than maist,
There's whiles I dinna ken,
A raw o' neeps is no a' like
An' why look for't in men?
Sae gin ye get your birse set up
By some dour cankert carle,
Content yersel'! For min' it tak's
A' kin's to mak' a warl'!

DROGGIE

Yersel' is't? Imphm! Man, that's bad!
A kin' o' thinness o' the blude?
Gaed aff las' nicht intil a dwam?
Keep's a'! But that's rale nesty, Tam!
An' lossin' taste noo for the dram?
(An' may it dae ye muckle gude!)

Noo! See the libel! "Thrice a day
A tablespunefu' efter food."
Drogues is nae better than they're ca'ed?
Some drumlie-like? Losh! ye're a lad!
The taste'll be byordnar' bad?
(An' may it dae ye muckle gude!)

Weel, here's your mixtur'—auchteen-pence,
I'd mak' it cheaper gin I could.
For beast or body maist fowk ken
Best's cheapest at the hin'er en',
An' on my drogues ye may depen'.
(An' may they dae ye muckle gude!)

Forgot your siller? Hae ye though?
Ye're in a richt forgetfu' mood!
Gie't ye on tick? I ken ye fine?
An' whustle on my fingers, syne!
Lat's see that bottle! Here's your line!
(An' may it dae ye muckle gude!)

THE WEE DRAP

He's a muckle man, Sandy, he's mair nor sax fit,
A size that's no' handy for wark i' the pit,
But frae a' bad mis-chanters he'd aye keepit free
Excep'in' that nicht he'd a fire in his e'e.

He was lyin' an' holin' at wark at the face,
For the gaffer had gi'en him a gey dirty place,
Sae while i' the gloamin' I sat owre my tea
He lowsed an' cam hame wi' a fire in his e'e.

Ae wife says "Saut butter," ane "Sugar o' leed,"
An' anither says "Poultice the back o' your heid"!

He first tried them singly an' syne tried a' three,
But sairer an' sairer got Sandy's sair e'e.

Wi's heid in blue flannen (he couldna stan' licht)
I'se warrant he lookit a bonny-like sicht,
Till dang near deleerit, as hard's he could flee,
Eck ran to the smiddy for ease till his e'e.

The smith was a billy wha cam' frae the sooth,
An' was awfu' sair fashed wi' a sutten-doon drooth.
He claimed half-a-mutchkin as fore-handit fee,
An' syne yokit howkin' in Sandy's sair e'e.

The p'int o' his gully an' sleeve o' his sark
Was a' the smith's gibbles for surgical wark.*
For ae fire extrackit the smith pit in three,
Till Eck was fair rackit wi' pain in his e'e.

At last to the doctor he gangs daft wi' pain,
An' gets a gude sweerin' an' syne some cocaine.
The fire was ta'en oot then, to Sandy's great glee,
An' he spent the neist week wi' a drap in his e'e.

---

* The rough-and-ready method of removing a foreign body from the eye was to loosen it with the point of a knife, and then draw the sleeve of the operator's flannel shirt across the eyeball.—DR

THE TRICKSTER

'Twas the turn o' the nicht when a' was quate
An' niver a licht to see,
That Death cam' stappin' the clachan through
As the kirk knock chappit three.

An' even forrit he keepit the road,
Nor lookin' to either side,
But heidin' straucht for the eastmost hoose
Whaur an auld wife used to bide.

Wi' ae lang stride he passed her door,
Nor sign he niver gae nane,
Save pu'in' a sprig o' the rowan-tree
To flick on her window-pane.

"An' is this to be a' my warnin', Death?—
I'm fourscore year an' four,
Yet niver a drogue has crossed my lips
Nor a doctor crossed my door."

"I dinna seek to be forcy, wife,
But I hinna a meenute to tyne,
An' ye see ye're due for a transfer noo
Frae the Session books to mine."

"At ilka cryin' I'm handy wife,
Wi' herbs I hae trokit awa,
An' weel ye may dae's a gude turnie, lad,
That's dune ye ane or twa!"

"At the hin'er en' Fair Hornie then!
Fair Hornie lat it be!
An' Govy-dick! ye can tak your pick
O' the ways fowk chance to dee!"

He rattled them owre till weel on fowre
An' the cock gae signs o' life,
On ilka ill he spak' his fill—
But nane o' them pleased the wife.

"Wi' siccan a ch'ice ye're unco nice!
Hoots! come awa, woman!" says Death,
"Gin ye canna wale ane o' the fancy kin's,
What think ye o' 'Want o' breath'?"

Noo, Faith! the auld jade was a humoursome taed,
As an auld wife weel can be,
An' she leugh sae sair at his fleechin' air—
It fairly gart her dee!

Wi' a gey teuch sinon in your neck
Ye'll lang keep clear o' skaith,
But the craftiest carle in a' the warl',
An' the kin'liest whiles, is Death.

THE DEIL AND JOCK MACNEIL

O, siller's gude an' siller's braw
An' puirtith ill to thole,
But dear's the price o' gaithert gear
Gin the price should be your soul.

Sae be ye laird or be ye caird
Or yerl o' high degree,
Lay by the wark ye hae in han'
An' herken weel to me,

While I shall tell o' Jock Macneil,
A smith o' byous skeel—
O dule an' wae, it a' cam frae
His dealin's wi' the Deil!

For Jock had made an awesome pack,
An' by't he maun abide,
That gin he was the foremost smith
In a' the kintra-side,

Ten gude lang year to hammer on
An' blaw his smiddy coal,
Ten gude lang year to gaither gear—
The Deil should hae his soul.

Ae winter's nicht when flecks o' snaw
Cam spitterin' doon the lum,
As stiddy rang nae blythe voice sang,
Jock wrocht's gin he was dumb.

Nae blythe voice sings as stiddy rings
When the he'rt is fu' o' wae—
Nine year an' mair had past, an' noo
But seven short months to gae.

O, the smiddy door flang open wide
Wi' a blast o' the gurly win',
An' leadin' his mear a bairdit man
An' auld cam stoiterin' in.

"Noo whaur gang ye, ye silly auld man,
O, whaur gang ye sae late?
The track to the foord is smoort wi' snaw,
An' the burn's a roarin' spate."

"An' wad ye mell wi' my affairs?
Far, far, am I frae hame!
It's miles ayont I bude to be
Had the white mear no' gane lame."

"I amna thrang, it taksna lang
To shoe an auld white mear,
See, pit that feed aneth her heid
An' set ye on that chair.

"Noo what be ye, ye silly auld man,
Noo what be ye to trade,
An' what can ye lay in my han' to pay
For this shoe that I hae made?"

"A saunt am I frae Heaven on high,
I hinna gowd nor gear,
But I can grant your he'rt's desire—
Three wishes ye may speir,
An' wi' the wishes I'll pay ye, smith,
For the shoein' o' my white mear."

"There's a pear-tree oot i' the gairden there,
Ye canna see't for snaw,
I wish whae'er may sklim intil't
Bides till I say 'Awa!' "

"A grant, a grant! O feckless wish!
Wi' fear my he'rt's opprest!
Twa wishes yet ye hae to speir,
An' dinna forget the best!"

"D'ye see that chair ye're sittin' on,
Wi' the lang an' gizzent back?
Whae'er sits on't e'en lat him sit
Till I bid him rise an' walk."

Up rase the saunt afore he said,
"O fule, ye stan' confest!
Aince mair a grant! But ae wish left!
Noo, dinna forget the best!"

"See, here's a purse het frae my pooch,
A purse o' linkit chain,
May a' livin' things that creep intil't
At my biddin' there remain!"

"O, I maun rise, an' I maun rin,
An' I maun saddle an' ride,
An' I maun reach the yetts o' Heaven
This nicht whate'er betide,
For ye've tint the best that man can wish
At the ca' o' earthly pride!"

'Twas a braw, braw nicht, weel on in hairst,
Wi' niver a breath o' win',
When Jock was switin' owre his darg
An' the Deil cam dannerin' in.

"It's a fine nicht, Jock," says the muckle black Deil,
"An' it's a' that, Deil," says Jock,
"What kin' o' weather has't been doon-bye,
An hoo is a' your folk?"

Auld Hornie girnt, "I hinna come
For a lang twa-handit crack:
Lay by that wark ye're warkin' on
For I maun hist me back."

"E'en lat me finish this gude horse shoe,
Syne I'm at your comman',
An' ye can try thae pears ootbye
That's hingin' to your han'!"

"I'll lat ye finish that gude horse shoe
As ye hae it in han',
An' I'll slocken my mou' wi' the bonny wee pears
Till ye're at my comman'."

As throw the winnock he keekit oot
Jock saw wi' unco glee
The Deil eat a' that he could rax
Syne sklim intil the tree.

"I hae ye noo, freen' Nickie Ben!
I hae ye by the horn,
An' the auld pear-tree shall be your bed
Till the cock craws in the morn!"

O, sair the Deil he tried to flit,
He banned wi' a' his poo'er,
He warselt weel, but ne'er a fit
Frae the pear-tree wan attour.

"Anither ten year, a bargain fair,
Ere I sit wi' ye in hell,
Shak han's on't owre this yird-fast stane*
That's stannin' by the well!"

Anither ten year o' gaitherin' gear,
Anither ten year o' pride,
Jock lookit roon' ae braw hairst e'en
An' the Deil was at his side.

"Ay, aince again your tack's rin oot,
An' this time nae denial,
For a full ten year I've grantit clear
By the shadow on the dial!"

"E'en lat me finish this braw horse shoe
An' that's a' my deman',
While ye can try thae pears ootbye
That's hingin' to your han'."

"O, I winna fash wi' pears the nicht,
I'm some distraucht inside,
I thank ye kindly—a' the same
It's here I'm gaun to bide."

"The while I finish this braw horse shoe,
The wark I hae in han',
E'en tak the chair ye see owre there,
Ye weel may sit as stan'."

Doon sat the Deil intil the chair
Wi' the lang an' gizzent back,
In sudden fear he strave to rise
An' niver a mudge could mak.

"I hae ye noo, Auld Nickie Ben,
I hae ye by the tail,
An' ye shall sit till the dews o' morn
Pits pearlins on the kale!

"Ye needna flyte, ye needna ban,
Ye needna rug an' tear,
Or I raise my finger an' bid ye walk
Ye're thirlt till the chair!"

"Anither ten year'll I gie ye, Jock,
Gin ye but set me free,
An' I'll pey ye back at the en' o' the tack
For the chair an' the auld pear-tree."

Anither ten year o' gaitherin' gear,
Anither ten year o' pride,
An' Jock stude still wi cockit lug
As the Deil stept saft ootside,

Syne yokit till his shoe again
Wi' dirdum an' wi' din,
But ae ee on the smiddy door
As the Auld Ane sidled in.

"Twice hae I come to tak ye, Jock,
An' twice ten year ye've thieved,
Thrice wi' the glam'rie o' your tongue
I winna be deceived!"

"E'en lat me finish this wee horse shoe,
An' I'm at your comman',
An' ye can try thae pears ootbye
That's hingin' to your han'."

"O, fruit's no gangin' wi' my he'rt,
Nor yet wi' my inside,
I'll no say but ye wish me weel
But here I'm gaun to bide."

"Then while I finish this wee horse shoe,
The wark I hae in han',
What ails ye at the chair owre there?
Ye weel may sit as stan'."

"My feet is cauld, I winna sit,
It sets me better to stan',
The while ye finish the wee horse shoe,
The wark ye hae in han'."

"O, a' folks say ye're cliver, Deil,
That unco things ye dae,
Ye can mak yersel' as muckle's ye like—
Noo tell me is that sae?"

He has swall'd himsel', an' better swall'd,
As the wind swalls oot a sail,
He has swall'd himsel', an' better swall'd
Till ye couldna see his tail,

He has sookit in air, and he's sookit in reek,
He's sookit in soot an' stour,
Till his horns gaed cracklin' throw the roof
An' his hurdies throw the door.

"Ye winna beat that," roars the muckle black Deil,
"Lang, lang, altho' ye try,
I can best ye there, my gallant smith,
An' I'll han'le ye yet, forbye!"

"Man, for the poo'er to dae siclike
I wadna gie a curse—
Lat's see ye mak yersel' as sma'
As creep intil this purse."

Nae horny-golloch is sae sma'
As the Deil's noo made himsel',
Intil the purse o' linkit chain
He's creepit heid an' tail.

Jock's snappit the purse o' glist'rin' steel,
The purse o' linkit chain,
He's leuch to hear Auld Hornie squeal
To be latten oot again.

"I hae ye noo, Auld Nickie Ben!
I hae ye hide an' hair!
An' I'll ding ye harns an' horns an' hoofs
Till ye binna sweir to swear
That aye frae here ye'll bide awa,
An' herry me nae mair!"

Wi's hammer he's dang him harns an' hoofs
An' horns an' hide an' hair,
Till he's passed his word as Yerl o' Hell
He'd herry him nae mair.

Noo, at lang last the smith grew nirlt
An' frail, an' fu' o' years,
Till ae cauld nicht he sough'd awa
Like the feck o' his forebears.

An' when he cam to the yetts o' Heaven,
O, wha is stan'in' there,
Wi's lang, lang baird, but the silly auld man
That aucht the auld white mear.

"Ye needna fleech nor yet beseech
Nor mak nae prayers to me,
For ye didna wish the ae best wish
When ye was offered three."

Jock heard it a' an' turned awa
An' hooly gaed his pace,
As he traivelt doon the weel-trod track
That leads till the Ill Place.

An' there he saw the yetts set wide,
Set wide against the wa'
While Symie's brookit bourachie
Was playin' at the ba'.

The Deil glowrt thrice ablow his han'
When Jock he did espy,
Syne stappit twa fingers intil's mou'
An' whustl't them a' inbye.

He's clashed thegither his iron yetts
Wi' dirdum an' wi' din,
He's chackit the tails aff a dizzen wee deils
That was late o' scram'lin' in.

"Na! A' my folk they ken ye, Jock,
Ken ye an' a' your gear,
Sae we're seekin' nae pears, an' we're seekin' nae chairs,
An' we're seekin' nae purses here!

"For ye arena fish, an' ye arena flesh,
Nor gude red herrin' are ye,
Wi' the Orra Folk at the Auld Cross Roads
Is whaur your stance maun be."

It's no a place ye'd ca' a place
Whaur Jock bides year by year,
In hopes o' pittin' anither shoe
On Peter's auld grey mear,
An' wishin' the ae best wish o' a'
Gin three he's gien to speir.

Sae be ye caird or be ye laird,
An' be ye sick or weel,
Whate'er your kind, bear aye in mind
The fate o' Jock Macneil.

For siller's gude an' siller's braw
An' puirtith sair to thole,
But dear's the price o' gaithert gear
Gin the price should be your soul.

The above is a free rendering in verse of a Scots folk-tale which was a favourite recitation of the late Professor Crum Brown. It is a variant of one of the many 'cheat-the-Devil' stories current throughout Europe, a good—if elaborated—Flemish example being given by De Coster in *Smetse Smee.*—DR

* A bargain made over an earth-fast stone was of old held to be specially binding.—DR

THE MILESTANE

A milestane's aside the road,
Like me it's gey an' aul',
Ye'll easy mak oot a' it says
For a' it says is "twal";
Ay, twal mile to some toon
Whauriver it may be,
An' be it twal or twenty mile
It's a' ane to me.

O' woman's love I niver kent
An' weel it was for her—
An' me, for some gey randies
Sticks closer nor a burr.
It's fine to ken I'm by mysel'
Wi' a lane weird to dree,
An' twal mile frae some toon,
It's a' ane to me.

My hame's whaur nicht may find me,
Gin folks lat weel alane,
An' tho' there's routh o' little else
There's routh o' ling an' stane,
For I was born aside the road
An' by the road I'll dee,
Be't twal mile frae some toon
It's a' ane to me.

TIME WAS

(1926)

"Time was"—in the Gaelic he thun'ert
Wi' the air fu' o' stour,
Frae the brods that his twa nieves had duntit
For mair than an hoor—
"When the weemin o' this congregation
Could sit on their hair"—
An' his een, like a gled's, seekit a' gait
For shingl't heids there
Regairdless o' Paul's holy flytin'
On earlier flirts—
"But noo they will no' find it easy
To sit on their skirts."

The kirk skailt, an' traivellin' hamewan
At Sabbath-like pace,
While the men said the words o' the preacher
Was pang-fu' o' grace,
The weemin o' that congregation,
Gey mim-mou'd an' grim,
At the back o' their minds wasna thinkin'
Sae muckle o' him.

THE SIBYL

Jock Tod was gey sma'-boukit
An' Meg a strappin' quean,
But when he speirt her mind o' things
The answer sune was gi'en,
"Och, ay! I think I'll tak ye, lad,
I'll tak ye jist because—
Weel, a' that I can see o' ye
Is a' there iver was."

Noo, i' the uptak, Jock, puir sowl,
Was niver unco gleg,
He scartit at his tousy pow
The while he glumphed at Meg;
He turned the maitter owre, an' syne
Says he, "I wudna fret,
For a' that there may be o' me
Is a' ye'll iver get."

39

They went throw life thegether
And shared its smiles and froons,
To find the warl' gey like themsel's—
A thing o' ups and doons.
Sae, at lang last, when Jock gaed aff
Feet foremost owre the brae,
Meg grat, "Weel, a' I had o' him
Was a' there was to hae."

THE SHORT CUT

Is't me ye're seekin'? O, ye're on the hike?
An' makkin' for Auldadam? Was ye, though?
An' they had tell't ye it was fairly warth the while
To tak a path, a short cut, like,
That lands ye at the toon an' saves a gude three mile?
An' that the shepherd—ay, that's me!—
Would pit ye on it gin ye speirt at him?
Imph'm!
Wha tell't ye that? O, ay, the merchant,
The mannie at the shoppie doon the road?
(Gin I had but his craig in thae twa han's
I'd rax it for him weel!
The hunker-slidin' bleck!
The coorse ill-deedie chiel!
He's ne'er forgi'en me owre that bogie-roll
I handit back till him a twalmont syne
Stinkin' o' ile, an' wi' a bittie twine
Fair i' the he'rt o't—the wee clarty swick!
But, fegs, there's ane can conter's ilka trick
An' that ane's me!
Weel does he ken it, sae he tries to lowse
A' thae bare-leggit limmers on the hills
To gar my yowes
Play helty-skelty; but wi' a' his wile
I'll live to see him yet whaur he should be,
An' that's the jile!)

The path, is't, lassie? Dod, it's growin' dark
An' gey an' like a gude ding-on o' rain!
O, ye're no feart at rain? Ye often hike?
Losh, lassies noo hae bigger he'rts than men!
Ye're used wi' gaun alane? Heard iver folk the like!

Ye hae gude title, lass, to wear the breeks
E'en a thocht langer than ye dae the nicht.
The path, ye said? Weel, when ye're at the brig
Haud fair up throw the plantin' on your left
An' dinna heed altho' ye hear some orra skreeks—
It's jist the owls: ay, naethin' but the owls.
What's foshen them? To get their suppers, lass!
They've mair adae o' nichts than sit an' sleep:
That plantin's fairly hotchin' fu' o' mice,
Ye'll fin' the deid leaves sotterin' under fit:
A rale divert it is the wey the craturs cheep!
Hoo big's the plantin'? Weel, noo, lat me see—
Ten meenutes' traivel easy taks ye throw,
Wi'oot ye hae to bide an' scoug the rain.
Syne, aince ye clear the trees ye'll see a knowe—
It whiles gies oot a queer uncanny shine:
I've heard my grannie say that lang, lang syne
A man, his wife an' bairns a' took the pest
An' dee'd, for nane would iver come them near.
Sae a' the neebors happit yird an' stanes
Owre the bit hoosie, oot o' mortal fear,
An' in the knowe, there, lies their puir white banes,
By nicht my collie winna pass it. Na!*
His birse gets up an' he aye taks the hill,
I winna say but what he fears some ill
An' sees some ferlies maybe best unseen,
For beasts hae sicht that bodies arena gi'en.
O, ay! ye say it may be nocht but fancy,
Yet fine ye ken the tales the auld folks tells
That gars ye deem a place a thocht unchancy.
But dinna lat that hinder ye, my lass,
Jist keep the Deid Knowe weel on your richt han',
Syne even forrit till ye see a cairn
Pit up whaur Tam the Tinkler foonert i' the snaw
In fifty-twa.
There's some'll hae't his ghaist gangs up and doon,
But that's jist blethers, lassie, tak't frae me,
For them that follows fraits, fraits follows them,
An', ony way, the path leads to the toun
An' saves a gude three mile.
Imph'm!
But see ye keep the path for ony sake!
There's some richt nesty bog-holes whaur ye'd droon
As easy as a kittlin in a pail,
An', fegs, ye wouldna be the first by twa or three!
But, ach! ye canna miss it wi' an ee
As gleg as yours.

41

Sae aff ye set afore it comes black dark—
Gude nicht to ye, my dawtie: ay, gude nicht! . . .

Hey, lassie! Hey! I clean forgot the bull!
Noo, wisna that unmensefu' o' me, noo?
Gin ye'd chanced suddent on him i' the mirk
I would hae blamed mysel' for't a' my days.
He's whiles a richt ill-trickit kin' o' wratch
An' whiles he's no': ye niver ken his tune;
He coupit owre a wife twa year come June
An' broddit a' her hips; but ach! they say
She skirlt an' ran awa frae'm up the brae,
A thing that weemin-folk should niver dae
For, tak't frae me,
A bull's best faced an' lookit i' the ee.
He's maybe no' on this side o' the hill,
But still
I'd pooch that big reid gravit, for it's ill
To tell the whauraboots
O' sic stravagin' brutes.
But dinna lat him hinder ye, my lass,
That path'll easy save a gude three mile.
Imph'm!
Na, na! Nae thanks! Ye're welcome! It would be
A weary warld gin we tint the chance
O' daein' an antrin kindness noos an' ance;
I aye like helpin' folk; ye ne'er can tell
When maybe ye'll be seekin' help yersel'.
Sae tak the path, my lass, for it'll save
A gude three mile.
Imph'm! . . .

Wull she? Nae fears! I ken the cut o'r fine!
Thon airt'll niver gar her werrucks stoun!
Nae mair than has't wi' ony o' the lave
O' shauchlin' hauf-cled besoms that's been shewn
The short cut to the toon.
She winna fash the yowes!
Thae jades is a' sic-like;
Gie them a tale o' hoolits, hauntit knowes,
Bogles an' bulls, an' twa-three cheepin' mice,
Syne a' the haill clanjamphry keeps the pike—
An' hauds weel i' the middle o't forbye!

* A reference to the many tales still told of cases where, in the days of the Black Death, the infected house was knocked down upon the unhappy inmates and then covered with earth and stones.—DR

THE PHILOSOPHER

Dinna look for muckle
An' ye'll no be disappintit,
Dinna think ye're somebody
Because ye're dooble-jintit;
Jouk an' lat the jaw gae by,
Tak a'thing as it comes,
An' niver wyte the grozer buss
For no' bein' fu' o' plums.

A' your gear's aneth your cap?
See ye haud a grup o't!
Gin your cogie's coupit
Ye yet may save a sup o't;
Jouk an' lat the jaw gae by,
Tak a'thing as it comes,
An' dinna wyte the grozer buss
For niver bearin' plums.

THE PHARISEE

"Lookin' roon' on the warl',"
Said the craw on the riggin',
"There's ae thing I dinna haud wi'
An' that's sornin' an thiggin'.
Thiggin' an' sornin',
Reapin' wi'oot sawin',
Comin' oot ilka mornin'
Beckin', booin' an' blawin'.
Thanks be, I'm no' like some folk!
I wark for my livin',
An' niver haud nae troke
Wi' ocht fleein' under heaven—
Ay, I'm speakin' o' you,"
Said the craw til the doo,
"Sittin' there on the wa'
Wi' nae heed o' the snaw,
Preenin' an' prinkin'
Wi' your 'Ruckity-coo,'
Eatin' an' drinkin'
Till your kyte's pang-fu'.
Thinkin' ye're o' the gentry,
Sae jimp an' little-boukit,

Pridefu' o' the entry
At nicht intil a dookit.
Weel could I pike your een oot,
Ye wee figure o' fun!
For a' the gude I've seen o't—
Beak an' claw an' feather—
May the fairmer an' his gun
Dae awa wi' ye a'thegether.
I'm scunnert to sit aside ye—
Ye're for aff? An' Deil guide ye!"

Crack-ack!
"What's *that* lyin' on its back?"
Speirt the doo at the snaw,
"It looks unco black—
Dinna say it's the craw!
Beak an' claw an' feather,
Fair awa wi't a'thegether.
Ye auld figure o' fun
Wi' your jokes aboot a gun!"

THE PRECAUTION

Scatter the mools owre him,
An' stramp them weel in;
It's oor chance noo to lay his heid low
As he did to mony in his day,
The sleekit nabal.
We're no' seekin' him up again—
Bonniest, aye, was the back view o' 'm,
Tho' whiles no' that easy to get.

But we'll pit up a heid-stane till 'm—
It'll maybe be safer,
Wi' a buttery bittie or twa on't,
For he aye likit fleechin'.
Syne, if his ghaist taks to daikerin' aboot
The sicht o't 'll haud him again,
An' he'll turn on his heel, weel-pleased like.

Ay, it'll cost a bonny puckle siller
An' he's no warth it.
Still, it's maybe safer i' the hin'er en'.
For he was a sleekit nabal,
An' nane o's is seekin' a sicht o' 'm again.

The original underlying idea of the laudatory tombstone was to placate the deceased, and so keep his spirit quiet.—DR

THE SEELIE KNOWE

Ye ken the Seelie Knowe, upbye, as ye gae throw the glen?
I niver pass the placie but my hair stan's fair on en',
An' I hae to haud my bannet on frae loupin' i' the air,
For ony airt's unchancy when the Gude Folk's there.

I've seen me pass it singin' as a curn o's gaed hame,
But when ye're a' your lee-lane ye dinna feel the same,
Ye mayna haud wi' bogles when the can'les burns bricht—
It's anither kin' o' story i' the wan mune's licht.

I mind ae nicht a twalmont syne, an' nae word o' a dram,
Gaun skippin' like a mawkin frae a muckle blackfaced ram,
I'd hae sworn 'twas Auld Geordie as his horns show'd owre the
Knowe
An' my he'rt was near ca'ed aff its stalk ere I wan throw.

There's maybe no' a word o' truth in a' the auld wives say,
Still I'se warrant it's no chancy, e'en in the licht o' day,
For what's the richts o' onything it's byous hard to ken—
But when I pass the Seelie Knowe my hair aye stan's on en'.

45

ELSPET

Aye, a' her life, afore she beddit
This was her prayer, as Elspet said it,

"Poo'ers o' the air! Be gude to me!
Keep me livin'—lat ither folks dee!"

It cairrit her on till eichty-four,
An' the wolf ne'er girnt at Elspet's door.

A'body trimmelt that catched her ee,
There niver was muckle she didna see.

The lasses a' held her in deidly fear,
There niver was muckle she didna hear.

What een and lugs couldna bring till'r hoose,
Elspet niver wad fail to jalouse.

Ilk ane gae her a ceevil gude-day—
When they fand they couldna get oot o' her way.

Ilk ane gae her a cheery gude-e'en—
When sooth-rinnin' water row'd canny atween.*

When the miller's mear had her fore-leg broke,
A'body kent the beast forespoke,†

A'body kent it was Elspet's spells
And a'body keepit the fac' til theirsel's.

Elspet niver gaed near the kirk,
Naebody likit to meet her at mirk,

An' the nicht the ase-puckle set fire till her chair,
A hare slippit bye wi' its hurdies bare.

Twa herds saw it and heard it squeal
As it hirpled awa for the aid o' the Deil.‡

But dee'd she in grace or dee'd she in sin,
Her gear a' went to her next-o'-kin,

An' shewn fast in till a lurk in her coats
Was an auld leather bag fu' o' gowd an' notes.

But the far-awa freen that was served her heir
Was slain in a tuilzie at Lowrin Fair.§

Aye, a' her life, afore she beddit
That was her prayer as Elspet said it,

"Poo'ers o' the air! Be gude to me!
Keep me livin'—lat ither folks dee!"

* A witch cannot pass the middle of the first running stream: south-running water is specially efficacious.

† 'To forespeak' is to give undue praise to 'beast or body', and is associated with the idea of 'The Evil Eye'.

‡ The witch could change into the form of a hare, and injury done to it was done to her.

§ 'Ill-gotten gear carries nae blessin'.'—DR

PAULINE'S POILU

I'm sittin' smokin' at the door
In shadow o' the gean,
An' he'rknin' till oor youngest ane
Bein' hushabyed by Jean.

It's a rale bonny peacefu' spot
An' dear it is to me,
Yet my thochts rins back at antrin times
To days in Picardy.

Ay, French folk is frem folk?
Well, frem e'en lat them be!
But I kent a lass or twa oot there
Was nane sae frem to me.

There was Léonie an' Jacqueline
An' Marguerite an' Claire,
Ay, faith, gin I tak time to think
There's maybe twa three mair.

O, fairly! What o' Rosalie
An', best o' a', Pauline?
She took my fancy easy
For she mindit me o' Jean,

An' cairrit me a bit owre faur—
It a' comes in a crack!

A simmer's day, the auld barn wi'
The orchard at the back;

The sunlicht tricklin' throw the leaves
Fell flickerin' on the wa',
An' the flourish o' the aipple-trees
Cam' floatin' doon like snaw,

While ilka man o' oor platoon
Sat strippit till the waist,
An' seekin' owre his flypit sark
To see wha'd catch the maist.

I'd dune gey weel, an', slippit on,
My sark was quater noo;
I took the fag doon frae my lug
An' stuck it in my mou',

Lit it, an' startit for the lade
To gie mysel' a dip—
An' by the gate there stude Pauline
Wi' ae han' on her hip.

The tither held a stalk o' girse
An's by 'r I socht to win,
She rax'd it oot an' kittled me
Jist fair aneth the chin.

Weel, what wud ye hae dune yersel'?
I kissed her on the mou'—
An' syne I had a veesion o'
A muckle French poilu!

Wha ca's the French a shilpit race
Ne'er spak a bigger lee,
For in his stockin's that same lad
Stude weel on sax-fit-three.

Tho' he was ong-permissy-ong
He'd nae permit to gie
To Pauline for to cairry on
Wi' chaps like you or me.

An' sic-like names he ca'ed the lass!
Ye'd thocht the man was daft;
Syne roon' he swang an' landit me
A lasher on the chaft.

He loupit here, he loupit there
An' aye anither wap,
While's ae fit catched ye square ahint
The tither ca'ed aff your cap.*

An' noo it kin' o' cam' to me
'Twas maybe some unchancy
To lat a muckle Frenchy see
Ye kissin' his financy;

For aye as I lat oot at him
I seemed to get his fit,
An' a' the boys was cryin' him on
An' lauchin' like to split.

Syne, like a bull, he chairged reid-wud—
I didna like 't ava,
An' joukit while his heid gaed thud
Richt throw the auld clay wa'.

Swack was the lad: like win'mill sails
His legs wrocht throw the air,
For he was smoort wi' stour, an', fegs,
He'd plenty o't in there.

We tuggit at his tunic
An' we ruggit at his breeks
Till oot he cam neeze-neezin'
As gin he'd rive his cheeks.

But Pauline took him weel in han'—
She fair pit on the branks,
An' makkin' 't up wi' him that nicht
Cost me near twenty francs.

For doon till the estaminy
The pair o's bude to gang
To please the lass, an' ile her chap's
Intimmers wi' vang blang.

Ach, weel, I hope he's to the fore
An' mairrit on Pauline—
Supper? I'm mair than ready for 't;
A'richt, I'm comin', Jean!

* The reference is to *la savate*, demonstrations of which, more or less successful, used to amuse our troops in France.—DR

THE FAREWELL

Haud up the gait, haud doon the gait
An' see an ye can find
Amang them a' a winsome may
Mair suitit to your mind;
Ay, doon the gait or up the gait,
Or ony gait ava,
Ae boon alane hae I to crave—
Frae my sicht haud awa!

THE OPTIMIST

"There's nae sin in a merry mind,"
Quo' the wifie cheerily,
As she gaed whustlin' ben the kirk,
An' rale jocoe was she,
"There's nae sin in a merry mind,
Na, nane ava that I can find,
There's nae sin in a merry mind,"
Quo' the wifie cheerily.

"O, lippen til't, aye lippen til't,"
Quo' the wifie cheerily,
The time she loupit owre the burn
As hamewan traivelt she,
"O, lippen til't, aye lippen til't,
To loup, your coaties ye maun kilt,
An' lippen til't, aye lippen til't,"
Quo' the wifie cheerily.

"Gude nicht an' grace an' muckle o't,"
Quo' the wifie cheerily,
As she gaed toddlin' aff to bed
Wi' sleepy twinklin' ee,
"Gude nicht an' grace an' muckle o't,
The warst o's hae a puckle o't,
Gude nicht an' grace an' muckle o't,"
Quo' the wifie cheerily.

THE WATER O' ANNAN

As I gaed doon by the Water o' Annan,
Readin' a buikie by Geordie Buchanan,
Little I gaithert o' what I was scannin',
Lang years syne.

Sodger was I, but the sword an' the cannon
Was oot o' my heid by the Water o' Annan,
Couthier things I was plottin' an' plannin',
Lang years syne.

Weel kent I that her faither was bannin'
Her an' me an' a' we was plannin',
Dannerin' doon by the Water o' Annan,
Lang years syne.

Nirlt wi' eild an' my back row'd in flannen,
My een canna deal noo wi' Geordie Buchanan,
Yet aye can I mind o' the Water o' Annan,
Lang years syne.

THE NEWS

Eh, mercy, noo, folk! Hae ye gotten the news
O' a' that's been happenin' up at The Hoose?
Keep me! If I iver heard sic a doon-fa'!
Weel, dinna lat dab an' I'll tell ye a'!

"She didna!"—"Ay did she!"—"It canna be,
Jean!"
"Says he"—"An' says she, than"—"Nae mair'n
yestreen?"—
"O, niver!"—"Ay, was it!"—"An' sae she's awa?"
Noo, dinna lat dab 'at I tell't ye a'!

There's a hantle o' things ye maun keep i' your loof,
Nae ilka affair can be cried frae the roof,
If they kent whaur ye got it they'd gar me look sma',
Sae dinna lat dab that I tell't ye a'!

THE LIKENESS

There was a Carse o' Gowrie wife
Wha'd reacht the winter o' her life
Wi' muckle toil an' gey sma' gain
Yet ne'er had had her likeness ta'en.
Ae nicht some kimmers, twa or three,
Crackin' like pen-guns owre their tea,
Gart sype intil the cratur's heid
The time was ripe to dae the deed.

'Twas lang, lang syne afore the days
When sic-like ploys is dune wi' ease,
An', sune as i' the place ye stap,
A's owre an' feenished in a clap.
Na, na! there's some o's, grey or beld,
'Ull mind the hardier days o' eld,
An' a' the routh o' artistry
The subjec' had to pit up wi'.

The mannie led her up a stair
An' set her in an elba-chair,
Syne posed her heid wi' yarks an' rugs
An' fixt a crook ahint her lugs,
Held up his han', cried "Noo, that's it!"
An' "Dinna move oot o' the bit!"
Syne joukit 'neath a velvet cloot
An' pu'd a funnel in an' oot.
First, as the wifie sat in state,
He fand he'd clean forgot the plate.
Neist shot he had at puir auld Meg,
The cratur crampit i' the leg,
An', while he's cursin' throw his cloot,
She bude to rise an' stramp aboot.
Sae at lang last when a' was dune
His face was like a nor'-wast mune,
An', sorry that she'd e'er begun wi't,
She'd switit aff gey near twa pun' weight,
Syne, feelin' she'd played well her pairt,
She dirlt hamewan in a cairt.

'Twas some gude whilie efterhan'
She keepit tryst there wi' the man.
At hame, her keekin'-gless was dim,
Wi' cracks that ran frae rim to rim,
The sun tried ilka day in vain
To warsel throw her winda-pane,
For aye his beams, despite their poo'er,
Was held wi' moose-wabs, soot an' stour,
An' sae, for years, like throw a haar
She'd viewed her veesage frae afar.

But noo she's han'lin' here her likeness,
Excitement gars her shak wi' weakness,
For, faith, it nearly owre did ca' her
To see hersel' as ithers saw her.
Speechless, at first, an' in amaze
On it she fixes a' her gaze,
Syne cries, while haudin' 't till the licht,
"That's me? Weel, that's a hum'lin sicht!"

NEEBORS

Ay, that's you, is't, doctor?
I thocht I saw ye comin' oot o' her hoose owre thonder.
An' is a'thing by?
Eh, but that's fine, noo; ye've had a sair hing-on!
Is't a laddie or a lassie?
Twins? Keep's a'!
But I'm no nane surprised—no' me:
She was aye a twa-faced besom.
I'm jalousin' baith the twa o' them'll favour *her*?
It winna be *him*, ony wey;
The mither'll be their nearest freen' in *thon* hoose;
A'body kens that.

What's that ye say? "Keep my tongue atween my
teeth"?
There's nae ca' for ye to be unceevil, doctor,
An' to a sufferer like me, tae!
I was jist speirin' for the woman—
As ony neebor would.

THE HEALIN' HERB

For ilka ill there is a cure,
Be it in root or leaf or floo'r,
An' aft-times roon aboot the door.

Tho' it grows free for a' mankind
Lang may ye seek afore ye find.

But for stark deid
There is nae remeid—
Nane.

The above deals with an old folk-belief.—DR

THE PACIFIST

Stop the fecht, for ony sake?
Na! no' me!
An' maybe get the reddin-straik?
Na! no' me!
I ken a trick warth twa o' that,
Gae try't yersel—I'se haud your hat,
But I'm no' sic a muckle flat—
Na! no' me!

Weel, rin an' fesh the bobbie, than?
Na! no' me!
I'm nane sae chief wi' a' that clan,
Na! no' me!
Fause witness, fegs, I widna bear,
But a' that I am keen to swear
Is jist, lad, that I wasna there—
Na! no' me!

ILKA DOG HAS BUT HIS DAY

Ay, laddie, as the years increase
An' frailties owre us creep an' creep
We hoast an' hirple till the ca'
To jine oor faithers in their sleep.
Thae knottit j'ints a' shot wi' pains,
That fobbin' as we breist the brae,
A' help to lat ye test the truth
That ilka dog has but his day.

Lang syne we warselt like the lave
Wi' routh o' hope an' scanty gear,
Gin ye made little o't owre-sea
I didna chance to best ye here;
An' noo we en' whaur we began
There aye is ae thing we can say,
For beast an' body it hauds gude
That ilka dog has but his day.

The game was warth the can'le, though?
Ye think it? Whiles I hae my doots
When a' the veteran has to tell
Maks lauchter for the new recruits.
Grey hair has lost its market noo,
Youth claims the richt to wear the bay,
But time tries a'; owre sune they'll ken
That ilka dog has but his day.

An' aye the queer auld game gangs on,
Man canna reist Time's turnin' wheel,
But see what helps ye ca' your gird
Is no' the black han' o' the Deil;
He'll len' ye spunk to gar it birl,
His road is plain-stanes a' the way,
But at lang last he'll learn ye weel
That ilka dog has but his day.

Na, naethin's new aneth the sun
Excep' whativer's clean forgot,
An' a' the battlefields ye win
Are owre the gr'und our faithers fought;
Sae tak't frae me, an' weel I ken,
Lie ye on feathers or on strae,
Ye'll fin' oot i' the hin'er en'
That ilka dog has but his day.

TINKLER PATE

They sat by the side
O' the tum'lin' water,
Tinkler Pate
Wi' his wife an' daughter.

Pate sings oot
Wi's back till a tree,
"Hurry, ye limmers,
An' bile some tea!"

Weel they kent
They'd hae cause to rue
Gin they conter'd him,
An' him hauf-fou,

Sae the wifie lootit
To fill the tin,
Slippit her fit
An' coupit in.

The daughter, gruppin' her,
Slippit an' a',
An' that was the feenish
O' baith the twa.

Heels owre gowdie
The pair o' them gaed,
Naebody cared,
An' naethin' was said,

But what Pate roared
As they made for the linn,
"Canny, ye jades!
Ye're awa wi' the tin!"

THE DEIL'S A BUSY BISHOP

Man, I was sayin' las' nicht to Jock
—A canny billy, that!—
There's heaps o' queer things happens noo
To gar ye won'er at;
O' godly thochts an' kindly deeds
The Lord gie us increase,
For the Deil's a busy bishop
In his ain diocese.

While a' the warld's sotterin'
Like tatties in a pot,
An' man's chief en' is naethin'
But to cut his brither's throat,
O' godly thochts an' kindly deeds
The Lord gie us increase,
For the Deil's a busy bishop
In his ain diocese.

Gin ye canna lo'e your neebor
Try an' lat the cratur be,
An' dinna yoke to whustlin'
When ye hear he's gaun to dee,
O' godly thochts an' kindly deeds
The Lord gie us increase,
For the Deil's a busy bishop
In his ain diocese.

I NE'ER SAW AUGHT WAUR
NOR MYSEL'

O, I hae been oot in a' weathers
An' I hae been oot at a' oors,
But spite o' auld wives an' their blethers
O' spunkies that murders and smoors,

O' bogles an' warlocks an' witches
To blast ye wi' curse an' wi' spell,
An' hunt ye owre dykes an' owre ditches—
I ne'er saw aught waur nor mysel'.

TAK' TENT

A reekin' lum's ill, but a wife wi' a raird
Is fit to gar ony man bite on his baird,
An' ban the bleck day he was iver ta'en in
By a yatterin' lump o' original sin.

Ay, wit is warth mair nor a well-turned leg
An' in walin' a wife ye hae need to be gleg,
What's dune in your haste ye've her lifetime to rue,
For she canna be unctioned alang wi' the coo.

When she's trampin' the blankets e'en gie her a scan
Sin' a mizzle-shinn'd maid is sma' use till a man,*
Aye kiltin' her coats i' the face o' the lowe
Wi' the bakin' an' washin' an' a' to ca' throw.

The auld carl said it, an' faith he's nae leear,
"Better the tocher that's in her than wi' her,"
A leal-he'rtit lass wi' a gude pair o' hands
Is mair o' a bargain than siller an' lands.

* 'A mizzle-shinn'd maid' is one whose legs have become pigmented by overmuch sitting in front of the fire. As a sign of laziness it has to be kept from the ken of suitors. The present fashion of short skirts and thin stockings is an aid to the mate-seeking male. 'Owre mony werrucks (bunions) to get a man' describes proverbially a second female handicap.—DR

ELFAN

O, ye will saddle the gallant black
As I shall saddle the bonny broon,
Frae aff oor shoon we'll shak the stour
O' this grey elritch toon.

For ye hae walked wi' chains o' gowd
To deck the doublet's cramoisie,
A smilin' face, an air o' grace
To mask black miserie.

Hame an' fame an' a' forgot
At the glance o' the Queen o' Fäerie,
An' ye've slept wi' your face to the mune, o' nichts,
Till scarce a styme ye see.*

But a' unkent I've busked your bed
Wi' dill an' vervain, thyme an' rue,†
An' I'll lead ye back to your lady's bower
Wi' he'rt aye leal an' true.

Aince mair ye'll breathe the caller air,
Aince mair ye'll hear her clear voice sing,
As the hoof-beats sound her heart will bound
To the rispin' o' the ring.‡

Pu' ticht the girths o' the gallant black
As eke will I o' the bonny broon—
O, master dear, lat's clear the yetts
O' this grey elritch toon!

* Moon-blindness.
† Anti-witchcraft herbs.
‡ 'Rispin' the ring' or 'tirlin' at the pin': running the ring up and down over the roughened staple of iron on which it was attached to the door, and thus announcing arrival.—DR

THE BELL

"Bide, lippen, thole,
Lippen, thole, bide"—
Whiles laigh, whiles loud,
As the wilfu' blast blew,
Cam' the bell as it jow'd
"A' I say is true—aye true
Frae the hippen to the shroud.
Throw a' ye hae o' life,
Bairnheid till eild
Or ye gang oot wi' the tide,
Throw its sturt an' strife
Haud fast an' dinna yield,
But bide, lippen, thole,
Lippen, thole, bide,
Lippen, thole,
Lippen."

DING DOON TANTALLON

Come awa, Bletherwin',
Come awa ben,
An' sae ye are back
To your calf-grun' again?
An' tellin's the story
Ye preach i' the parks
O'a land o' free a'thing
Whaur naebody warks.

An' what's your ain pickin's, lad,
What wad ye gain?
Fowre hun'er a year
Wi' free hurls i' the train!
Jist fancy a' that
For the gift o' the gab,
When ye connach'd gude leather
For 'ears as a snab.

Ye was foshen up here
In this placie o' oors
An' wha'd hae jaloused ye
A man o' sic poo'rs?
Cursin' the pollis
An' bannin' the Kirk,
Whaur nane o's wud lippen ye
Herdin' a stirk.

Come awa, Bletherwin',
Come awa ben,
A' your freens thocht
Ye'd the wits o' a hen;
Yet ye'll ding doon Tantallon,
Ae fine day ye pass,
An' big a braw brig o' 't
Richt owre to the Bass.

THE KNOT

A' the knots o' a sailor's craft
Weel could he tie in a trice,
An' nae thocht ava o' a day to daw
When the Deil wad han'le his dice;
Yet I stude yestreen at the back o' the kirk
In oor ain hame port o' Leith,
An' heard him tie ae knot wi' his tongue
That he winna wark lowse wi' his teeth.

A wacht o' wine for a leman's lips,
A guerdon at skreich o' day,
Syne a galliard's tale 'neath the bellyin' sail
Aince beards were saut wi' spray;
An' him the blythest blade o' them a'—
But he's bye wi't, sure as Death!
For Mess John's gart him tie wi' his tongue
The knot that 'ull better his teeth.

Ay, spunk lowes wan at a foul fire-en'
When your rudas rovin's bye,
An' a limmer's glamourie dims an' dees
As ye're hushin' her wirral's cry;
Fareweel, shipmate! that I thocht was mine
Sae lang as we baith drew breath,
An' a malison fa' on the tongue that tied
What ye'll never win throw wi' your teeth!

THE GUDE MAIDEN

Ilka auld wife was aye a gude maiden,
Brawly I ken it for aft am I tauld,
But awa to Auld Nick wi' their girnin' an' chidin',
It's eith to be sauntly aince bluid's rinnin' cauld.

They've a' had their fling wi' the lads o' their fancy—
Why suld they daunton a lassie like me?
An' say a' I dae is misleart an' unchancy;
Weel may they blaw aince their eildins a' dee,

Wi' nane left to gab o' the days o' their daftness
Or ever they crined wi' the cranreuch o' eild;
But bide till they're beddit! Awa wi' sic saftness,
I'm aff to keep tryst at a weel-happit bield.

THE OBITUARY NOTICE

Dod! An' sae *he's* awa, is he?
Some folks is awfu' for deein'!
That'll make fowre o' the Session, noo,
Slippit awa in sax 'ear.
Weel, weel, he was a gey lad in his day:
I could tell ye twa three bars aboot him,
Ay, could I,
An' richt gude anes, tae!

Ach! what o' 't?
Royt lads maks sober men,
An' young saunts, auld sinners.
Sae they a' haud, an' he was nae waur nor the lave.
Ony wey, the cratur's awa
An' here's a lang bittie aboot 'im i' the papers.
"Much respeckit member o' the community."
Imph'm.
"For mony years an elder, an' a J.P."
Jist to think o' a' that, noo!

Ay, ay, an' sae *he's* awa!
Dod, he was a gey lad in his day—
Some folks is awfu' for deein'!

YE COULDNA BLAME HER

She'd a tongue like the clapper o' the Auld Kirk bell,
Ach! ye couldna blame her,
For she aye had some new story she was yooky for to tell,
Sae ye couldna blame her.
She could redd up a' the parish or ye finished wi' your tea
An' faither a' the bairnies in't 'at cam a thocht aglee
Or tell hoo mony crans the herrin' boats wad get at sea,
An' ye couldna blame her.

She'd a tongue like the clapper o' the Auld Kirk bell,
An' ye couldna blame her,
For she kent a heap o' orra things the papers daurna tell,
Sae ye couldna blame her.
There wasna ony reistin' her aince she was in her stride,
For naebody she haltit, but ran on like time or tide,
An' wha was gaun to haud her when ye kent her man was fley'd?
Ach! ye couldna blame her.

She'd a tongue like the clapper o' the Auld Kirk bell,
An' ye couldna blame her,
Her 'at telt her neebors' denners jist by sniffin' at the smell,
Ach! ye couldna blame her.
For news o' a' the happenin's she'd aye a chronic thirst,
An' if ony was afore her an' she hadna telt it first,
I'se wad ye hauf a mutchkin 'at the cratur wad hae burst,
Sae ye couldna blame her.

TRACHELT

The wee trachelt cratur gaed shauchlin' throw the rain
An' the deuks an' the hens cam' skelpin',
While auld bawsent Bawtie loupit rattlin' at his chain
An' deavin' a' the lift wi' his yelpin'.
"Heeshty! Heeshty! Oot amang my feet!
I'm jamphlin' i' my bauchles an' it's dingin' on o' weet,
Od, life's a dish that's sizzont mair wi' bitter nor wi' sweet,
An' it's me's had a byous orra helpin'!"

The wee trachelt cratur's peelin' tatties by the fire
Wi' her skirly-nackits fechtin' an' greetin',
Syne up an' aff to milk the coo that's rowtin' i' the byre,
An' see till her beddin' an' her meatin'.
"Hist ye! Hist ye! Dinna be sae slow!
The trokes that's feenished up the stair leaves plenty
        mair below,
For woman's wark is niver dune an' naethin' for't to show,
It's a job, lass, that taks a lot o' beatin'."

The wee trachelt cratur's deid an' happit i' the yird,
An' the shools are dune wi' their fykin',
An' on a branch abune her there's a bonny-singin' bird
Whaur the sun on her bed-heid's strikin'.
"Wheeshty! Wheeshty! Bairnies, no' a cheep!
She's only new fa'n owre yet, ye maunna brak her sleep,
For she lippent till a promise that the Makar o't'll keep
O' a darg fully mair till her likin'."

THE PICNIC

Eh! Sic langwidge!
Onybody hearin' ye 'ull hae a bonny tale to tell
An' you a jined member o' the Kirk!
Think black burnin' shame o' yersel!
Wi' your mou fou o' sangwidge,
I won'er it disna choke ye,
Ye ill-tongued stirk!
An' a' this tirravee
Owre a drappie o' bilin' watter on your taes!
Keep me!
Dinna provoke ye?
Did onybody ever hear the like o't a' their livin' days!
Ye hae a gude neck!
Wi' twa mile o' sand to pit your muckle feet on
What gart ye stick ane o' them
In aneth the stroup o' the kettle?
An' what sorra else did ye expeck?

You an' your fit!
They're a perfeck scunner—
Baith the twa o' them,
Ay, an' has been ever sin' I kent ye.
A decent woman canna get moved at her ain chimblay—
cheek,
An' sma' won'er!
Hoo aften hae I telt ye I couldna get anent ye
An' you aye lollopin' thae dagont feet o' yours on the fender?
I whiles wish ye had widden legs,
They wadna be sae tender
An' they wad match your heid better—
Ay, wad they, fegs,
An' hae saved ye happin' aboot the noo
Like a craw wi' a sair inside.
Sit doon, man! See,
A' the fowk 'ull think ye're fou—
Here's your cuppie o' tea!

Oho! Ye're no' gaun to bide?
Ye've had a' the tea ye're wantin'?
An' ye're no seekin' ony mair o' my clatter?
Weel, awa an' tak a bit paidle til yersel,
Gin ye maun be gallivantin'
Try the watter.
The sea 'ull maybe cool your temper
An' your taes as weel.

But mind ye this o't!
I've taen your meesure,
My bonny man, aince an' for a',
An' this is the hin'most time
I'm oot for a day's pleesure
Wi' you—ay is it!
For I'll stan' nae mair o' your jaw!

Ach! You an' your fit!

THE BONNIE LASS O' MAGGIEKNOCKATER

Noo, the sizzon bein' Spring, it's the time to rise an' sing
O' a lass that I ha'e likit exterornar,
An' the first time that I met her it was owre at Fetterletter
When I coupit her by breengin' roon a corner.
Losh! She made a rare to do, for she thocht that I was fou,
An' tell't me my condeetion fairly shockit her,
But I swore her accusation hadna ony gude foundation
An' soothed the bonnie lass o' Maggieknockater.

> Ay, man, ay! Ony time ye're stappin' by
> Look in an' gie's a cry an' tak' a look at her,
> Ye'll notice she's a' there an' gey little waur o' wear,
> The teuch an' bonnie lass o' Maggieknockater.

Man, the things ye recolleck when ye sit doon an' refleck
On the worries that beset ye on Life's journey,
Ay, things that in their sizzon nearly gart ye loss your rizzon
Ha'e slippit doon the road to Hecklebirnie.*
Tak' that waesome nicht in June we was lookin' at the mune
When a muckle lump o' gundy near-han' chockit her,
Till I daddit on her spine, an' cried "Say 'ninety-nine'!"
An' saved the bonnie lass o' Maggieknockater.

An' there's ae nicht I recall at a Grand Subscription Ball
An' a happenin' that sent me near dementit,
For jist aboot half three, ony netteral micht see
That the fiddler an' his tune was ill acquentit.
Sae my lass says, "Sic' a crime! Can ye nae gie's better time?"
An' the drucken cratur flang the eicht-day clock at her,
Syne a dizzen o's an' mair was a' whammlin' on the flair
As weel's the bonnie lass o' Maggieknockater.

Ay, Spring's the time to sing, baith for birdies on the wing,
An' for lads that's nae sae souple i' the thrapple,
Yet each lass ye sing aboot is in stracht descent, nae doot,
Fae the wife that founert Adam wi' an apple.
But tho' Time gaes birlin' on an' a hantle years ha'e gone
Since her mither in the cradle first had rockit her,
I'm aye richt gled I met her thon nicht at Fetterletter
An' pleased the bonnie lass o' Maggieknockater.

* Hecklebirnie is ten miles on the other side of the Ill Place, according to folk-lorists.—DR

A PER SE

Aiberdeen an' twal' mile roon,
Fife an' a' the lands aboot it,
Ta'en frae Scotland's runkled map
Little's left, an' wha will doot it?

Few at least 'at maitters ony,
Orra folk, it's easy seen,
Folk 'at dinna come frae bonny
Fife or canny Aiberdeen.

AT THE SIGN OF THE BLUE PILL

'Je prends mon bien ou je le trouve'

FISHING

It was in the old, happy, pre-war days, when it seems, looking back, there was more time to do things and more pleasure in doing them. A friend and I had set out from Cromarty in a fishing boat, rowed by two weather-beaten local worthies, to make for the inlet to the Firth and there indulge in an hour or two's line fishing.

As we pulled lazily out, Stroke jerked his head towards the coast and said, "There is a big cave there."

"Hugh Miller's cave," added Bow.

"Ay," acknowledged Stroke, "Hugh Miller's cave. And if you go in there and keep on you will come oot seeven miles inland."

"What?" I exclaimed.

"Weel, weel, that is what Hugh Miller says in a book, anyway. Ay, he says it in a book. I have seen the book."

"There's a heap o' lees tell't in books," remarked Bow with great truth.

"Maybe," said Stroke; "but that is in Hugh Miller's book."

"Ay," Bow agreed with gloom; "it is in his book right enough;" and he spat—I thought somewhat contemptuously—into the ocean.

"But who," I asked, merely for the purpose of enlivening the conversation, "was Hugh Miller?"

"Shut up!" said my friend, *sotto voce*, but savagely.

"You will not have heard of Hugh Miller?" asked Stroke; "to think of that, now!"

"He was a here-aboots man," Bow remarked, explanatorily.

"Chee-ology," elaborated Stroke; "stanes, ye ken."

"Ah!" said I.

"And there is a museum he colleckit in Cromarty. Och! there is a heap o' stanes in that museum."

"There will be a coup-cairt-fu' o' stanes there," said Bow.

"There will be twa coup-cairt-fu's," said Stroke; "it is a big museum."

"And what if there is?" queried Bow. "It is not every one cares for stanes: one stane is very like anither." And he spat again, even more contemptuously than before.

Then, for an hour, with a dropped anchor, we fished with fair success until my friend succumbed to *mal de mer*, unrelieved by the well-meant consolation of our crew.

"There is nothing," remarked Stroke, "so good for the stomach as being seek."

"Nothing," agreed Bow; "it clears the system of all kinds of pisons. Oh! it is a fine thing for you: a very fine thing indeed!"

But my friend never uttered a word until we were coming back again and were opposite the cave.

"Ay, ay!" said Stroke, quietly reminiscent; "that will be Hugh Miller's cave."

"Who," I commenced—

"Shut up!" said my friend for the second time; "if you start that business all over again, I warn you that I shall be ill on top of you!"

For safety's sake I refrained: but in Cromarty it is a mistake to say that a prophet is without honour in his own country.

ON NAMES AND NAMING

One of the most curious straws which show how the present-day winds of public opinion are blowing us away from the dear dead days of Queen Victoria is the change which has come over the methods of inserting notices of births and deaths in our daily papers. Marriage notices still remain much the same, and are at their nadir in May, thus demonstrating the eternal grip of superstition on the fair sex and those who follow after them.

Now, in the days gone bye, if the average citizen—whom we can perhaps most safely and accurately call John Dud—had an increase in the number of his family, it was duly chronicled, simply, naturally, and as a clinical fact: "The wife of John Dud of a son." Of course, it might be "of a daughter", or "of twins, son and daughter", or "twins, boys", or "twins, girls", or, once in a way, "of triplets", the sexes being duly detailed. But the point is that no insult was held to have been levelled at the lady by calling her merely the wife of John Dud, and, looking at it from the legal point of view, there was no obtrusive claim of parentage on the part of the said John Dud. In which there was some wisdom, if we hold by various old saws.

But of late years the feminist business has sprung up like a fungus and complicated the whole affair, interfering unduly with the simplicity—and obvious truth—of the old-time Victorian notice. Nowadays, in the shorter variety of the reformed method, we have: "To Mr. and Mrs. John Dud, a son" (or otherwise, *v. supra*). This, of course (again looking at it from the legal point of view), is not so entirely safe as the Victorian notice, taking such notice as a mere statement of fact.

A further extension is: "To Mr. and Mrs. John Dud (*née* Widdershins), etc." Of course, the French feminine should prevent you thinking it was John Dud, as well as Mrs. Dud, who was born Widdershins; but, personally speaking, I am always a little confused about it—every time.

Still, that is not so bad as the more determined attempts to shove John Dud into the background altogether. One method is: "To Aspasia Gladys (*née* Widdershins), wife of John Dud, etc." This successfully dims the personality of poor John and puts Aspasia, his spouse, in the limelight, where, dear soul, I have no doubt she wants to be.

But on the occasion when John gets a regular "K.O." and meets his matrimonial Waterloo the notice runs thus: "To Aspasia Gladys (*née* Widdershins), M.A., B.Sc., M.B., Ch.B., D.P.H., D.T.M., wife of John Dud, a daughter (Mary Wollstonecraft)." Here you have really to look for John before you find him at all. You feel that the reference to John Dud should have been put into brackets as well. He has had it duly advertised to his world that he is not a university man, that he is merely a citizen of no credit and renown, who, doubtless, dare not tap the ashes of his pipe out on the bars of his smoking-room fire at night without the monthly nurse coming down to inquire acidly if he is aware that the patient (M.A., B.Sc., etc.) is trying to sleep. I am always truly sorry for John when I meet him in the above guise on opening my morning paper. And I am certain that Mary Wollstonecraft Dud when she attains years of discretion (and a vote) will second her mother in seeing that, as our American friends would say, "Pop stays put."

And the sadness of it is that if the poor man had lived forty years earlier Aspasia Gladys (and all the rest of it) would merely have been his wife! John's only chance of a small place in the sun seems to be the formation of a society for reintroducing the *couvade*.

Now, take the death notices, and the disinclination of the lady (even when dead) to figure as a widow. Supposing Mrs. Dud survives the aforesaid John, she will leave directions that she is to be "put in print", not as "widow of the late John Dud", but as "wife". Why? What—in spite of the elder Mr. Weller—is wrong with a widow? Is it now held to be a term of contempt? In the good old days she would not even have been "widow of", but "relict of" the late J.D., and "prood o' the fac'", although the word has a ruinous suggestion about it.

The next step will probably be that should the unfortunate John Dud (on whose behalf, I trust, your sympathies have now been enlisted) die as a widower, his daughter (Mary Wollstonecraft) will insist on "papering" him as "husband of the late Mrs. Aspasia Gladys Dud (*née* Widdershins), M.A., B.Sc., M.B., Ch.B., D.P.H., D.T.M." So that poor John, to the bitter end, will carry the burden of his temerity in having married into the brainy family of Widdershins, and have his inferiority complex flung after him into the great beyond.

THE DOCTOR O' FIFE

A Medical friend has put in my hands the following old Scottish song. He declares that it has been in the possession of his family for several generations, and that his grandfather held the belief that the song went back to the days of "Davie Lyndsay". I think myself that this claim is far-fetched; for although it possesses all the *naiveté* and rural frankness of the older Scottish verse, the use of the word "doctor" instead of "leech" (and several other more modern touches) almost certainly places it in the seventeenth (or early eighteenth) century. The refrain at once suggests an air similar to (or the same as) "The Cooper o' Fife"; while the reference in it to "Jamie Sympsone", in spite of the archaic spelling of the name, makes one suspect either a modern interpolation or even an entirely nineteenth century origin. When one considers the case of "Hardyknute" and the downfall of the then ballad experts, it makes one doubly cautious in accepting the verses at the valuation placed on them by my friend. I trust he will take these criticisms in good part, for I should be the last man to under-estimate the value of his old manuscript, as a vivid description of some of the manifold woes of the rural practitioner even at the present day.

(1)

There was an auld doctor wha stoppit in Fife,
Calomy, lodomy, noo, noo, noo,
An' a shepherd had ca'd him ae nicht till his wife,
Wi' a hey Lucina! And ho Jamie Sympsone!
An' a' the carfuffle o't, roo, roo, roo!

(2)

Noo the shepherd was auld an' the wife she was young,
An' they said he was sair hauden doon wi' her tongue.

(3)

"Ye'll hae to come up wi' your drogues an' your airns,
For I'm thinkin' ere mornin' she's gaun to hae bairns."

(4)

The doctor cursed an' the doctor swore,
But he muntit his mear an' he rade frae the door.

(5)

The roads they were bad, an' the weather was waur,
An' he sune was bejaupt to the hurdies wi' glaur.

(6)

When he gat to the hoose at the heid of the glen,
He tethert his mear an' he strode awa' ben.

(7)

He strode awa' ben but he heardna a cheep,
For the wifie was beddit an' soond asleep.

(8)

Noo the sicht o' her kin'lt the doctor's ire,
For the shepherd had tell't him the lum was on fire.

(9)

Sae he rax'd her a thun'erin' skelp on the doup,
An' the wifie sat up wi' a skreigh and a loup.

(10)

Nae signs o' labour were there to be seen,
An' the os was the size o' the heid o' a preen.

(11)

Quo' the wifie, "What was't ye was led to expeck?"
"O, gin I'd the shepherd I'd thraw his auld neck!"

(12)

"Ay, dinna blame me, sir, but pit in on Jock,
For he sat a' the e'enin' an' glowrt at the knock.

(13)

An' when that the hauns had gat roon' to hauf ten,
He gruppit his bannet an aff doon the glen.

(14)

But what was his erran' he never lat on,
An' little I thocht 'twas for you he had gone."

(15)

The doctor cursed an' the doctor swore,
But he muntit his mear an' he rade frae the door.

(16)

Noo, gey sair dune wi' the win' an' the rain,
The shepherd was pechin' his road hame again.

(17)

When he keppit the doctor, "An' hoo is the wife?"
"Ye fule, she's as weel as she's been a' her life!"

(18)

"Eh, doctor, man doctor, ye'll hae to come back!
For ye ken its her time by the almanack!

(19)

Just come awa' back, sir, I'll show ye the score,
For the nick-stick's hung at the back o' the door!"

The doctor he rax'd him a cut wi' his whip,
An' he left the auld cratur a-birsin' his hip.

(21)

'Twas anither three weeks or the shepherd cam' doon,
Wi' the swite halin' doon like the rain till his shoon.

(22)

"O, its I'll rin roon for the mear till the stable,
For ye'll hae to come up, sir, as quick as ye're able!"

(23)

"Haud on," quo' the doctor, "lat's hae a' the facks!
Is this some mair o' your almanacks?"

(24)

"Na, na," quo' the shepherd, "For I was to tell
That this time the wife had sent for ye hersel'!"

(25)

The doctor cursed an' the doctor swore,
But he muntit his mear an' he rade frae the door.

(26)

An' when he gat till her he fand for his sins,
He'd to bide sax hoors while the wifie had twins.

(27)

When they tell't the auld shepherd he ruggit his hair,
"Noo, hoo the wide warld's she gotten a pair?"

(28)

Quo' the doctor, "For rizzon ye needna gang far,
When you think what a twa-faced deevil ye are!"

Now, in the song, whatever age it may be there are some discrepancies to be noted by the curious in such matters. For example, verses 3 and 27 are mutually contradictory; in the former the shepherd evidently anticipating a plural birth, in the latter expressing surprise thereat. But this may have been subtly introduced by the writer to emphasise the diagnosis of the harrassed and irate doctor in verse 28. Verse 10, again, is obviously a modern interpolation; no early song-writer would have been so definitely clinical in his facts. The mention of the "nick-stick" in verse 19 is of interest, for it is still common in Fife, Berwickshire, and other places, when a matron's calculations are wrong, to say "She maun hae lost her nick-stick", the reference being to the old notched tally-stick, the predecessor of the almanac, used by herdsmen and shepherds. The metaphor used in verse 8 is still a stock one in rural Scotland under the circumstances mentioned. The doctor's conduct in verses 4, 15 and 25, is not entirely unknown at the present time even in these days of motor transport; but his action as described in verse 9, on first interviewing the shepherd's wife, is quite out of keeping with either the Victorian or the modern obstetrician, and would tend to put the authorship of the song back to ruder times. But however all that may be, I give it to you as I got it, and the erudite reader must form his own conclusions.

FROM THE CHINESE

China is much in the news just now, and it has struck me how very little genuine interest we take in that country's literature. Most of us are thoroughly conversant with the works of Confucius, and many of us have at least a nodding acquaintance with Lao Tsu. But why stop there?

In "Over Bemerton's" E. V. Lucas airily introduces us to Chang Chih-ho, Chao Fu, Chen Shih, Sun Fang (who was a philosopher, and not, as you would imagine, a dentist dealing largely in shiny gold fillings), Yin Hao, and several others. But it is curious to note how little, if any, attention has been given to the poet Televius; in fact (but I stand open to correction) I am unaware of any previous attempt having been made to translate his works.

So far as can be gathered he flourished—if any true poet can be said to flourish—about a hundred years after the death of Confucius, to whose works he was probably indebted to no small extent for his profundity of thought and philosophical outlook; a fact that was in all likelihood duly and unfavourably commented upon by the literary critics of his day. For there is no greater sin than plagiarism, or anything approaching to it.

And yet, the suspicious, ferrety mind which is always on the outlook for another fellow's "cribbing" is not of too high an order. When *The Princess* came out, Tennyson was, if not pained, at least considerably annoyed by a Canadian noting the curious coincidence that four of his lines very closely resembled another four in Shelley's *Prometheus*. Whereupon the poet wrote to his critic somewhat testily. "I do not object to your finding parallelisms. They must always occur."

Of course they must, even amongst the deepest thinkers: just listen, on the next opportunity, to half a dozen proletarians discussing, with the necessary verbal adornment, whether that famous Irish hero O'Dumphy should have shot for goal with his left foot instead of heading the ball. Each borrows intuitively from the diction of the other, and all draw upon a common stock of words and ideas. So with poets.

But in reasoning with the Canadian, Tennyson went further afield. "A man (a Chinese scholar)," he says, "some time ago wrote to me saying that in an unknown, untranslated Chinese poem there were two whole lines of mine almost word for word."

The interest here to me, of course, is whether or not the untranslated poem referred to was the work of Televius. One can at least say that it might or might not have been; but beyond that no scholar would care to go.

Now, of the life of Televius little is known. His original name, as derived from his ancestors, was Bung Fu; and in his youth he was the prey of dissolute habits. But finding these incompatible with the successful carrying out of his occupation (that of an itinerant dealer in porcelain), he abandoned the drinking of spirituous liquor, became a rigid temperance reformer, and, taking to literature in place of drink, assumed the pen-name of Televius.

To render, from the original Chinese, a truly idiomatic translation, giving what one might call the full flavour of the poet, is not easy. But his line of thought may be gathered, even if dimly, from the following excerpts, which at least show how little the nature of man has changed throughout the ages.

Many people,
And these not the most silent in the community,
Claim to have an open mind.
But make the grave mistake
Of having it open at both ends,
So that their acquaintances are distressed
And depressed
By hearing and feeling the wind blow through it
With a hollow and dreary whistle.

It is quite evident that he had been in close touch with leading politicians, and had possibly made a study of the works dealing with the economics of his day. But he is equally at home with the gentler side of domestic life.

It is well
That thou shouldst greet the day with a cheer.
But if, after a restless night,
The wife of thy bosom
Has just then got thine offspring to sleep,
Be not thou surprised
Should she fail to chorus thy gaiety.

And how profound, how humble, and yet how full of commonsense are the following lines:

When, in the self-complacency of youth,
I looked around on my fellow-creatures,
I was overjoyed that such remarkable oddities
Had been provided by the gods for my entertainment.
But now, in the serenity of age,
I am at times uneasy
Lest the high death-rate
Long prevalent in my district

> May not be at least partly attributable
> To the effects of the politely suppressed derision
> Of those who have been regarding
> Me.

Spring cleanings, evidently, came within his ken; for he sings feelingly:

> Strange indeed it is
> That even the gods cannot plant
> In the heart of woman
> The faintest understanding of the value
> And sanctity
> Of manuscript, new or old.

Probably on account of its carminative effect, Confucius has told us, "If thou wouldst live long and be happy, eat much ginger." And I think his influence can be traced in the following lines of Televius:

> What are the plaudits of the crowd
> But wind?
> Has it gone to thy head?
> Then haste thee to the leech,
> Whose drugs will direct it
> Whither it should go.

Which, in turn brings us in touch with a saying of a Central African tribe whose name has momentarily slipped my memory, "Take care of the bowels and the brains will take care of themselves." And this sane view is corroborated by that now much neglected American philosopher, the late Mr. Josh Billings, who laid down the valuable dictum that "a good outfit of bowels was worth any amount of brains". I wish, for the advantage of our race, that all Directors of Education (who can never agree upon a definition of what that popular fetish "Education" really is) would study the works of the deceased Josh.

But however that may be, let me conclude my comments on Televius by giving you this:

> Both the philosopher
> And the thief
> Deal with abstractions.
> How unjust it is
> That only one of the two
> Should end in the hands
> Of the public executioner!

ON THE TRIALS OF COUNTRY PRACTICE

The following story has the double merit of (a) being true and (b) coming from Fife. (I do not wish, of course, to insinuate that this is unusual.) Old lady to her doctor, "Ay, I've haen fifteen a 'thegither, and I was aince sent to Edinburry to be cut for a tumour." What became o' the tumour? "Weel, if ye wish to ken, it's just turned twenty, and if ye look ootside ye'll see't atween the stilts o' the ploo." It had been "ane o' thae gaitherins that comes to a heid without poulticin'", as another worthy dame in "the Kingdom" once remarked to me. All of which shows that even doctors may sometimes be wrong.

I suppose most of us at times wonder how, failing, as we sometimes do, to supply the general demand for infallibility, we manage to hold practices together at all. To be a successful general practitioner only three things are required—the temper of an angel, the patience of Job, and the power to work miracles. And yet how few of us possess the necessary triple qualification. For myself, I am working hard to get number two, with small hope of attaining numbers one and three.

The average patient has the idea of the savage that death is not a natural thing, but is caused by evil spirits—panel doctors and things of that sort—

> 'Tis the story they tell of poor Hodge in his shell,
> Or the peer in his family vault,
> Had he lived—well, 'twas just what he ought to have done
> But he died—'twas the doctor's fault.

For the chief use of a doctor in the community is that some people may swear by him and the rest swear at him. There is no *via media*. I remember an old Scots farmer I once knew many years ago who, at our first meeting, looked me up and looked me down, and then said, "Weel, I houp you and me'll get on." I told him I hoped so too. "Ye see," he continued, "it's this way wi' me, if a man's a freen' he's a freen', and if he's an enemy God peety him." Luckily for me we became "freen's".

In token of his friendship he offered me his services as a judge of horse-flesh when I went, as a purchaser, to a horse fair. (In his own gentle, diplomatic way he told me that "I wid be a' the better o' somebody wi' me that kent the difference between a horse and a haystack.") He drove me to the seat of war in a dogcart with a very spirited young horse in the shafts, and on the way we called at a neighbouring farm to pick up the tenant thereof. My friend and I were in the front seat, and the other man got up "ahint". Unfortunately the horse started with a jerk—"lat a breenge forrit", in fact—and the passenger behind promptly fell out on his hands and knees. Whereupon the driver, pulling up, looked over his shoulder and said, "Losh, man, I thocht ye said ye was gaun wi's."

A LUNATIC

I often wonder if general practice is quite as lively as it used to be: my own experience makes me think it is not. Indulging in that mental exercise called "looking backwards", I came to the conclusion the other night that time gone brought one a bigger catalogue of curious happenings.

In one dear old country town of happy memory—a town of one straight cobbled street the better part of a mile long—I remember one quiet summer (and Sunday) morning being wakened to get a message from the local Inspector of Poor to go at once to see a man who was ill. That was all the message: no details. I arose and went to the address given. The patient lived by himself in a house down a "close" opening off the main street, a small house that stood by itself in a garden. When I arrived I knocked at his door, and the owner, a large, bearded, and brawny salmon fisher, opened it, grunted "Ay, it's you, is it?" and let me in, locking the door behind him. I followed him into a combined living and bed-room, which looked as if a very comprehensive free fight had recently taken place there. Pictures hung askew on the wall, with the glass smashed; an old grandfather's clock had its face "ca'ed in"; and a four post bed—an extraordinary relic of someone's better days—had its roof tilted badly through one of the uprights having developed an acute angle in the middle of it.

Well, they were a lively lot in that town on occasion when Saturday night came round, so I merely thought at first that he had been having a few friends in and had not had time to "redd up". Sitting down on a chair by the fireside with the patient doing the same opposite me, I noticed—still without perturbation—that he was fondling a large axe on his knees, while I asked him the usual preliminary "What's the matter?"

"Matter?" he observed; "there's matter enough to my way o' thinkin'! Look at the picturs! Look at the bed! Look at auld uncle Georgie's eight-day knock!" And then he muttered to himself, "And he's speirin' what's the matter!"

"Well," I said, "who's done the damage?"

"Fine ye ken that," he replied. "It's thae d----d electric wires sending me messages from Dr. T. at C. Ilka time a message comes I hae to get up and smash something wi' the axe: and I'm aboot tired o' this, for I've been at it the better pairt o' the nicht!"

Now I knew exactly where I was! Dr. T. of C. was the superintendent of the County Asylum. My friend and fireside companion of the axe was evidently "a person of unsound mind"; and I was shut up and locked in alone with him at 4 a.m. on a Sunday morning when every living soul in the place was in the arms of Morpheus.

"And what's mair," he continued impressively, "I'm thinkin' Dr. N. and you's mixed up in this business!" (I was, right enough: but Dr. N.—my "chief"—was soundly reposing on his virtuous couch.) So, taking a long breath, I went off at the deep end.

"You're right as regards Dr. N.," I said confidentially. "I've suspected him for a long time: it's a dirty piece of work, and we'll have to get him! Tell you what! Come on up with me and we'll get the bobby and collar him amongst us!''

"Come on!" he said. But when he got to the front door and—O joy!—unlocked it, he whispered, "Na! You gae for the bobby and bring him here, and we'll talk ower the best wey to nick the auld deevil!"

So I went off for the bobby, right enough, and we wired the Asylum; and when two attendants turned up some hours afterwards they and the unfortunate constable took the furniture destroyer away to where he belonged. *En route* he managed to smash every pane of glass in the hired conveyance.

But by that time I had gone—and very thoroughly too—for the Inspector of Poor, who had known all along that the man was "wud" and had not even troubled to let me know.

All the same it was a fine old town, and full of characters. That same bobby—peace to his ashes! for he sleeps with his fathers—was a huge man with a tawny beard. The great function of the year, there, was the annual fair, and a fair in those days meant "fechtin'"', otherwise it was, of course, no fair. When the street, late at night, was thronged with revellers, with a scuffle every hundred yards, the bobby used to save himself a lot of trouble (and assaults to the effusion of blood) by shouting out in a stentorian voice, "Whaur are they? Haud them there till I get at them! I'll sattle them!" And the contestants for the "croon o' the causey" generally melted into thin air: for he was a mighty man of valour.

THE TRIBE O' GALEN

The following ditty was sung at the annual dinner by one of our members, who is best left un-named. Some thought the air to which he sang it was "A man's a man for a' that", others that it was "Maggie Lauder". But most held it was a judicious mixture of both.

> As I was traivlin' through Steenhive,
> The nicht was growin' late, man,
> I heard the soond o' clatterin' tongues,
> An' knife an' fork on plate, man;
> Says I to Jock, "What is't, my cock,
> Are Germans in possession?"
> "Na, na," says he, "it's a gaithrin' o'
> The medical profession."
>
> "My sang," says I, "d'ye tell me that?
> What kin' o' billies are they?"
> "There's some," says Jock, "are fair and fat,
> An' some are thin and swarthy;
> There's some o' them are surgeons, an'
> There's some o' them physeecians,
> Wi' general practeetioners,
> An' twa-three obstetreecians."

"An' what will a' the toonsfolk dae
The nicht if they're nae weel, man?"
Says Jock, "they'll hae to keep their beds,
An' tak' a Beechem's peel, man".
"An' what aboot the wifies, noo,
If they be ta'en in labour?"
Says Jock, "they'll hae to ca' awa'
Wi' some auld skeely neighbour."

"Lat's stap inside," says I, "and mark
The tae kin' frae the tither—
Hoo would you tell a surgeon, noo,
Frae his physeecian brither?
Where a' seem keen upon the drink,
An' shovin' doon the crowdie:
Noo, tell me hoo a common man
Could single out a howdie?"

"Weel, lat's begin," says Jock, "an' note
The heid-mark o' a surgeon—
It's wi' the knife he saves your life,
An' nae wi' peels an' purgin'.
If ony o' them mak's a joke,
An' thinks ye dinna prize it,
He gies M'Burney's p'int a poke,
To duly emphasise it.

"Physeecians, noo, ye want to ken—
Ye needna be in doot, man—
Gin ye hae only gumption, lad,
Ye'll easy mak' them oot, man;
Just skin your e'e till two or three
Are fairly fou o' wine, man,
They'll fit their glasses tae their lugs,
An' cry, 'Say ninety-nine, man'."

"An' noo," says Jock, "I'll tell ye hoo
Ye ken the obstetreecians;
At ilka table aye they tak'
Left lateral poseetions.
Their hands a' shine wi' vaseline,
An' since the days o' Moses,
They aye pit up two fingers when
They're gaun to scart their noses."

Noo, I was awfu' sair impressed
Wi' a' that Jock had tel't, man;
My he'rt was duntin' in my breast,
Sic great respeck I felt, man.
An' when I saw them toddlin' oot
What time the thing was skailin',
Says I, "for honest, dacent folk
Gie me the Tribe o' Galen!"

BACK TO BENARTY

In looking over Scottish Song anthologies it is curious to note how many "single song" men there are. *E.g.*, the author of "The Boatie Rows", John Ewen (if it was John Ewen), has left us nothing else. It seems, then, that to erupt into one song and for ever hold one's peace (in that special line) is not uncommon. Amongst extremely minor Scottish "makars" we have the gentleman who, having compiled a volume of prose, handed it to the public in the earlier part of last century with this touching poetical foreword, his only effort in verse—

> Rin, little bookie, through the warld loup,
> Whilst I in the grave do lie, wi' a cauld doup.

Why he specially dwelt on the extra low temperature of one part of his *cadaver* as compared with the rest, history revealeth not further. But the old Fifeshire laird of Benarty, long gone to his rest, had the same fundamental idea in his little poem of rural contentment, also the only poem from his pen—

> O, happy is he that belongs to nae party,
> But can sit on his doup an' look oot at Benarty.

One can imagine the old worthy sitting of a fine summer evening at his open library window, sucking his yard of clay or tapping his snuff-box, content in his soul as he gazed on his hill, for, like the late Dr. Farquharson of Finzean, he "owned a mountain". I never see Benarty without thinking of him, although when I saw it last, surrounded by pitheads and a malcontent mining population, mainly "incomers"—not true Fifers—bent on the destruction thereof, I fear me much that, had he revisited the glimpses of the moon, he would not have rested so easy in his chair. And, at neighbouring Lochore, Syme would have said of his youthful home, even more sadly than he said it to "Rab" when he last went there, "No! No! This is not my Lochore!"

These fine old fellows, country bred, rich or poor, were much more contented in these bye-gone days, simply because their environment was more peaceful. Bicycles, motors of all kinds—especially that infernal modern Juggernaut, the char-a-banc—telephones, cinemas, etc., etc., all tend to seduce the country-man from the healthful habit of sitting on his doup and looking out at Benarty or whatever other decent hill a beneficent Providence may have placed there to catch and rest his eye. Contemplation of the right objects brings contentment, contentment cheerfulness, and cheerfulness the necessary charitable outlook on the motives of one's fellow-beings. Back to the land; back (if you will pardon me, and metaphorically speaking) to your doups; back to your Benartys!

ON MODERNISM

A compulsory few days in bed have led me to read a certain amount of modern poetry; I mean the kind of stuff that is being thrown at us just now by the "Incomprehensibilists". It is curious how that particular type of artistic and poetic lunatic persists; Bunthorne is never out of date. He is a plain-dealer according to himself; no flies on him! He describes life as he sees it, and if he is seeing double at the time, of course he describes it that way. Then if you can't see it as he describes it you are a Philistine, and your place is "outside the building, please", with the dogs and the rest of the doubtful catalogue.

One necessary part of the equipment of the incomprehensible clan is a large and uncouth vocabulary, while ordinary words assume new values, *e.g.*, a sunset "shrieks". What frightened it is not stated; possibly the poet reciting his own works. Changed times, anyhow. We used to be quite satisfied when

> The western waves of ebbing day
> Rolled o'er the glen their level way.

But evidently poor old Sir Walter hadn't got hold of his sunset at the right end. Gabriele d'Annunzio said some time and somewhere—I think it was before he got that fall on his head which let a lot of politics out and some religion in—that the ordinary man had a vocabulary of 800 words, while he (modest non-advertiser) had one of 15,000, which he had carefully culled from old books on agriculture, Machiavelli, Ovid, and other more or less modern and ancient authors. Well, in our honest old land, I suppose we have old books on agriculture; but who is to take the place, in our literature, of Ovid or of Machiavelli when we would go a-word-gathering to emulate the gifted Gabriele?

Queer folk they be, *sans doute*, and queer subjects they take—sordid and "dopey". Here is the kind of thing—

IN A CAFÉ

> Two of us—Yes! and another
> That is to say
> Three.
> Males merely, travailing in trousers.
> In silence we sit at the circular table
> Silent like us, stained and marble topped,
> And on it our glasses now emptied
> Of absinthe.
>
> Aye as we sat there
> Sniffing stale *caporal*
> Twice had the hour struck
> Ghostly and dead of tongue,
> While there was wherewithal,

Sombrely sipping,
Gloomed we with fish-like eyes at each other,
Or, hand over mouth, watched
The obese flies on the ceiling.

Dame!
Enter the woman—
And it was as if in a cellar
Someone had lit a candle
Driving the rats to their burrows,
The evil black rats to their burrows
In our subconscious selves.

Of the *demi-monde? Ah, oui!*
Un peu grisée and a slut.
Still, when she left,
Out went the light
And again scuttled the rats to and fro.

Encore une fois? Volontiers!
Another absinthe,
And another.
Rats?
Nay, but the bats now,
Hover and return
Back to their habitat—
The dear bats,
Our own bats,
The bats in our attics.

Or perhaps it may be some soul-lifting theme like this—

HAM

Ah!
Avid
For pabulum,
Pabulum for Gut,
Pabulum for Ghost,
Pabulum for Gut and Ghost,
I came near.
I was anhungered when I saw it
And its beauty held me
In all its streaky glory—
Old gold and ruby,
White, with crimson and rose.
It drew me to it in silvery, salivary ecstasy,
And Gut cried, "Ai! Ai!"
A ham? Yes!
Near but untouchable!
For while Gut cried
"Ai! Ai!"

84

Borborygmously booming,
Ghost said, "Avaunt,
And sully your soul not!
Behold! See ye not there the sunset?
Worshipful, wonderful—
O Sun! Hill-dipped and hidden,
Cuprosely refulgent!"

So, avid for pabulum
Yet orgulous in self-hold,
Behold me refraining,
Remaining,
Anhungered.

Thus, then, by the yard length,
Or, better mayhap, by the bushel,
Brim full and pressed down,
In sooth good measure,
With all the metaphors mixed
As the careless bibber mixes his cordials,
Tokay on Spanish, Spanish on Geneva,
Geneva on Rhenish—
Well! If this be poetry
I'd rather have the other kind,
Where you got an odd rhyme or two
With a decent lilt in it,
And could
Sing the damned thing!

Yes, after all, rather a relief to chuck the whole caboodle into the ashes,
light a pipe, and start humming—

As Dinah was a-walking in her garden one day,
Her father came to her, and thus he did say—
"Go, dress yourself, Dinah, in gorgeous array,
And get you a husband both gallant and gay."

Still, let us be open-minded and fair; what appeals to one type of mind
flits unnoticed past another. Not so long ago an Irish patriot—I forget
which variety, but he was in the hands of the police, anyhow—had on him—
"concealed about his person" is the legal expression, isn't it?—the following
deadly poem—

May God above
Send down a dove
With teeth as sharp as razors,
To cut the throats
Of English dogs
Who slew our Irish patriots.

It is somewhat difficult to analyse the composite feelings of the singer. He
starts with a pious wish that the bird of peace should descend from above.
Then his mood changes, and he fits out the poor bird more like a pirate junk

than a decent, easy-going pigeon, and with a denture contrary to all known ornithology. "Patriots" is not a really good rhyme for "razors", but, of course, he was writing in an alien and hated tongue; had he put it in Erse it would have gone swimmingly. And yet, after all, I have no doubt the finished product had had its admirers, and that its recitation had drawn tears from the eyes and revolvers from the pockets of not a few. Simple things appeal to simple souls. Many years ago a long-term convict, seized with the divine afflatus, scratched with a nail on a stone in his cell—

> Cheer up, boys!
> Down with sorrow!
> Beef today
> And soup tomorrow!

Now, *that* too has its merits. It is short; it is consolatory; the dietary statement was probably true. And, next time you feel a bit down in the mouth, just try the effect of repeating it. "It has dune me a heap o' gude" (as the old wife said when she first had a binaural stethoscope applied to her chest) on many occasions. Besides, it is so easily remembered.

A MEDICO'S LUCK IN THE WAR

Medical brass hats. On them alone I could write a book; not, mark you, to attack the Medical Service—which, taken all over in France, was as sound as a bell—but to deal with the impossible people. Some of these were only the happy-go-luckier members of the ever delightful "Fenian Brigade"; some were merely amiable cranks. But a few others, had they been horses, one would have labelled as vicious. But all of this class I met were fortunately amenable to appropriate and carefully thought out treatment.

One of them, whom I remember yet with maledictions mellowed somewhat by the passage of the years, dearly loved to descend suddenly on a Main Dressing Station when a push was on, and, oblivious of the fact that the O.C. had at such times to be on duty all over the place, express great wrath if that officer was not there in person to greet him respectfully on the threshold. From my office window overlooking the entrance I saw him one day jump from his car and dive into the old barn that was our Receiving Room, and immediately hastened across to meet him, arriving some thirty seconds after his advent.

"Well, you're here at last, are you?" was his genial greeting.

"Yes, sir."

"And now you *are* here perhaps you'll tell me what that ----- fool there" (pointing to an N.C.O. who was standing rigidly at attention and gazing into vacancy) "can't, and that is what the devil these two barrels are used for?"

I gazed into a corner of the barn and saw there on trestles two small barrels which I had never in my life seen before. But it was no use to tell him *that*.

"We were using them for barley water, sir, but we found it didn't keep well."

"Then why the blazes couldn't that fellow there tell me that at once?" And he consumed the unfortunate N.C.O. with his eyes. I, too, gazed at the culprit reproachfully for unnecessarily withholding information so evidently essential to the well-being of an inspecting officer.

When he had left after a tour of the show (where, curiously enough, seeing the mood he was in, he found fault with nothing else), I went to the N.C.O. and asked him what on earth the barrels were for and where they came from? He was an Englishman that I had on loan, and he answered—

"Most unfort'nit thing, sir, but these 'ere empty barrels was below a tarpaulin in the corner, and I had just 'auled the tarpaulin orf to see wot was there w'en 'e came in."

We conjointly examined the two derelict barrels with interest, and found one was labelled "Rum" and the other "Lime Juice!" They were at once removed and broken up for firewood, the sergeant very properly remarking, "Lucky job, sir, 'e didn't pursoo the subjick!"

Yes, he was a truly great man, that same happy warrior. Going round with him he would come, say, to the blanket store and rap out,

"How many blankets?"

It was, of course, impossible to say accurately without consulting the Q.M., as there was a constant come and go of such articles. But to reply "I'll ask the Quartermaster, sir," was fatal. His answer would have been:

"The Quartermaster be ----! You should know all the Quartermaster knows and a ---- sight more!"

So the result was that he always got an immediate answer of something like this:

"Eight hundred and seventy-two, sir, and fifteen under repair"; the sergeant-major chipping in with, "That's right, sir" (gallantly running the risk of having his nose bitten off for intervening); and the war was a step nearer being won.

On another occasion, when we were running a Corps Main Dressing Station during a push, with a very numerous personnel to look after, and the place going like a fair, a certain high-up medical mandarin sent in a demand for an immediate report as to why it was that so many safety-pins had been indented for on the Advanced Depot of Medical Stores the week before, with whatever further information on the nature, quality, merits, demerits and ultimate destination of the safety-pins supplied could be given. Safety-pins! Name of a pipe! All my work was laid aside for two hours while I concocted this report, and, with all humility, I can say truthfully that it was a work of art. The introductory paragraph, I recollect (and I managed to extend the report to two typewritten foolscap pages), ran thus:

"When considering the subject of safety-pins, it must always be borne in mind that the best are those which most nearly follow their prototype, the Roman *fibula*."

Then came a detail of (1) for what purposes we legitimately used safety-pins; (2) the illegitimate demands made on M.O.s of Field Ambulances and battalions for safety-pins by combatant officers and others not entitled to such luxuries; (3) the different manufacturers who supplied safety-pins; (4) the manufacturer whose products seemed specially reliable (more or less true); (5) the number of safety-pins supposed to be in each box; (6) the average number really in the boxes (probably true); (7) the average percentage of safety-pins which doubled up or became otherwise inefficient when used (possibly true); and so on to the bitter end, padded out with rolling Gladstonian periods, and really (although I say it who shouldn't) reading uncommonly well, if you took it as merely rather hurried journalism. And I remember when, somewhat wearily, I handed it over to be typewritten, I could not help thinking that the Germans had really got it in the neck this time, and that we were at last beginning to get a genuine move on in a prolonged and sanguinary war.

Later on my senior in the Corps, through whose hands it passed, and who was a thoroughly decent chap—he had Celtic blood in his veins—rang me up on the phone and said:

"I say! I got that report on the safety-pins."

"Yes, sir?"

"Never knew so much about safety-pins before!"

"No, sir?"

"It should settle him though." (Pause.) "Oh, by the way, send me a copy of your next novel when it comes out, will you?"

Mais que voulez-vous? A la guerre comme à la guerre! To do it was, of course, painful in the extreme, but what else could you do? If you were to be left in peace and the work carried through, that kind of chap had to be spoon-fed on flap-doodle simply to get him out of the road; he asked for it all the time, and the wise man gave it to him—in judicious doses.

I remember another senior genius in the Medical Service finding quite unwarranted fault with an officer in charge of a scabies ward at a Divisional Rest Station.

"What are you in civil life?"

"An oculist, sir."

"An oculist! Great Heavens! An oculist in charge of a scabies ward?" (Then to me.) "What the devil do you mean by putting an oculist in charge of scabies?"

"Only one other officer available, sir."

"Then, hang it all, put him on!"

"Very good, sir; he's a lecturer on physiology."

I thought he was going to throw three separate kinds of fit and then burst. But he only turned an empurpled visage on me and said solemnly:

"Now look here, this kind of thing's got to stop! D'ye hear? D'ye understand? Got to stop—got to stop at once! You'll look out an officer who's a *dermatologist*—a fellow who's made a special study of skins—chap who has done that sort of thing for years—*years*, mark you! And a junior officer with specialist qualifications too! Got that?—I'm going to collect all cases of scabies together at one centre, and *these men* are going to be in charge of them! See to it!" And in an atmosphere of "dammits" and growls he worked his sulphurous and saluted way to his limousine and departed.

Now you see "these men", as far as we were concerned, simply didn't exist: that was the worry of it: they weren't there! But Napoleon I said that difficulties exist for the purpose of being overcome, and Clausewitz gave us the dictum, "In war do the best you can." What annoyed me mostly on this occasion was that I was only acting A.D.M.S. for the real man on leave, and he had just gone the day before: it was not my *pidgin*: however, I supposed I could make a dermatologist or two out of nothing just as well as the next fellow, if I took the matter up seriously.

It so happened that in one of our medical units was an officer—a most efficient and gallant officer—who in the piping times of peace was a dentist. I went to him and told him that I meditated turning him into a dermatologist, and that I was genuinely sorry that I had to do this: it made me feel like a magician changing a princess into a rabbit. I also reminded him that he had known me well for years, and I was sure he would bear me out in saying that, *en civile*, camouflage, bluff, casuistry, special pleading and Jesuitical reasoning were absolutely foreign to my nature. I reminded him also of the developmental connection between teeth and skin, and that really, to a man with a scientific mind and the wider outlook, the ultimate difference was so slight that if a brass hat who knew nothing about either asked him about skins, he could quite properly reply that he had been doing "that kind of thing" all his professional life. But I told him I put no pressure on him; if he had a conscience he must not muzzle the thing to oblige me: these were matters for personal decision: I only asked him to remember that we were in the Army and that there was a war on. And next I hied me to a very smart young Canadian M.O., at that time attached to us, to whom I said:

"Don't correct me if I am wrong! I understand you were for two years house physician at Montreal Skin Hospital. On this understanding, or misunderstanding, I have appointed you assistant dermatologist at the Combined Scabies Station. The decision is final."

Well, the dentist and the Canuck, being sportsmen, took the show over and ran it with great efficiency and success; so efficiently that they were kept at the job long after they were thoroughly fed up with it. Two days after it was opened the great man came round to inspect.

"Ugh!" he grunted, as I met him at the door of the building, "what kind of a show have you got?"

"Very good indeed, sir."

"Humph! That's for me to say, not you! Got these skin men to look after it?"

I seized the opportunity to dodge the question and to introduce the officers to him.

"Know anything about skins?" he growled at the senior.

"I ought to, sir."

"Ought to? Why the devil ought you?"

"Done this sort of thing for twenty years, sir."

"And what about this fellow?"

"Montreal Skin Hospital, sir," drawled the Canuck, diplomatically avoiding any unnecessary misstatement of facts.

"Humph!" And then he turned to me. "And you were fiddling about with oculists and lecturers on physiology while you had these other fellows up your sleeve the whole ---- time! Organisation! The right man for the right job! It's what I'm teaching and preaching and you won't take it in! Just you remember this business in future as an example of what can be done when you put your mind to it."

And I said, "Very good, sir!" And I felt it too.

The officer with the chilblains is also a case of interest, although the hero of that tale was a dear, kind-hearted old chap. But I think his very arteries were made of red tape, and a Divisional or a Corps order was to him as unchangeable a decree as the laws of the Medes and the Persians. He was a good enough administrative officer, but all the medicine he had ever known had, long ago, run out of the heels of his boots. We were carrying on a Divisional Rest Station at the time, an institution where sick and slightly wounded were taken in for treatment; and if, after seven days, they were not fit to return to the line, were sent back to the C.C.S., being, *ipso facto*, struck off the strength of the Division. Well, one day a young officer came in who had nothing more or less wrong with him than very severe chilblains, and who was extremely anxious not to go further back, as he had temporary rank in his unit which he would thereby lose, while his O.C. was equally desirous of his rejoining.

But on the seventh day he was still unfit to go up the line, so we kept him on, gave his chart a touch of temperature, and trusted to luck. On the ninth day round came our old friend, buzzed cheerily through the wards and then came to the case of chilblains, whose chart he glanced at.

"Oh, hang it all! Look here now! This is too bad! Nine days! Surely you know the order about seven days being the maximum stay here? Send him down by to-night's convoy."

"I think, sir, we should exercise great care about removing this officer: it is an acute case of *erythema pernio*." (And let it be known to the laity that this is merely the Latin name for chilblains.)

"Oh, bless my soul! I didn't know *that* though! We would need to be a bit careful here—Eh? What? But look here—he has got no temperature to speak of!"

"Some of the very worst cases haven't, sir."

"Oh, well, glad you told me about this. *What* was it you said he had? Oh! Keep a careful watch on him! Take no risks! That wouldn't do at all!" And off he went, obviously musing.

Some days later he turned up, breezy and cheery. As he went up the corridor he said:

"And what about that acute case of ——? You know—that fellow with the ——? The case we couldn't move? How is he?"

"Much better, sir. I think he'll come round all right now."

"Dashed good job we didn't move him, eh?"

I respectfully agreed. And two days later Captain Erythema Pernio rejoined his battalion.

Of course every man has his fads, even the very best of us: I should not be at all surprised if some men who served under me thought that I had a few trifling weaknesses of that sort myself. One of my seniors was perhaps the most efficient, kindly, courteous, helpful officer whom I ever met in the Service. But he was death on thermometer-breaking, and at his conferences a most thorough explanation had to be given of all indents sent to the Advanced Depot of Medical Stores for such articles. The M.O.s of Field Ambulances, battalions, and other units, had to see to the filling in of weekly returns with the headings (1) Number of clinical thermometers broken. (2) By whom broken. (3) How broken, etc., etc. And I always remember the story told of one southron medical orderly, pouring out his soul on the form through the medium of a stubby pencil. "Under foloing circstances. Patent had thermomter in mouth when a shell burst in his visinty so he chewd on it." Which he chewed on—the shell, the thermometer, or the vicinity; likely bits of them all—is not clear, but the "patent's" conduct, "under the circstances", was excusable.

And then there was the incident of the rats: that was not a medical brass hat, though, but a "Q-monger". The iron rations of our unit had disappeared gradually, and our Quartermaster indented for 241—our total number—at one go-off, a somewhat wholesale order. And then "Q" started a correspondence which ran:

(1)

"Reference your indent of ---- for 241 iron rations. It is not understood how all your iron rations have disappeared. Please explain."

To which the Q.M. replied:

(2)

"Reference your (1). These rations have been lost mainly through the action of rats."

What he meant was that the rats had in many cases eaten through the linen bags in which the iron rations were carried, and that the tins had fallen out through the holes so caused while the men were on the march or in billets. (It was really a bit thin.) However, in came:

(3)

"Reference your (2). Please explain how rats can eat through tin."

Here the Q.M., with a troubled mind, brought the correspondence to me, and we tried them with:

(4)

"Reference your (3). It is pointed out for your information that the rat prevalent in the district is not the small black rat, but the large, grey Hanoverian rat."

The correspondence ceased and we got the rations handed over—"Q" had evidently not got a good text-book on natural history at hand.

"Ay, there's queer folk in the Shaws!" And that reminds me of less important people and the tale of "Wee Ginger", which is another kind of story altogether. Divisional Headquarters were at one time in a collection of huts set on a windswept hill, approached from the main road by a duck-board track set in a sea of mud. From 10 a.m. to noon I had held a medical board on men claiming to be unfit for continuing in the line; and at 12.30 I was going over the papers bearing on the cases seen. Suddenly the door of my "Armstrong" was opened and a man literally "blew in": for, as he turned the handle of the door the wind vigorously finished the operation and jerked him into the hut, all my papers whirling off the table. I asked him somewhat hastily, what in the wide, wide world he thought he wanted? He was a little man with large spectacles fixed in a clock-face visage, a Scottish bonnet roguishly cocked a-jee on a mop of red hair, a kilt well below the knees of a pair of Harry Lauder legs, and a general air, probably assumed, of childlike simplicity. He saluted slowly, like a mechanical toy, and asked me with mild interest:

"Are you the Boord?"

"Am I the *what?*"

"Are you the Boord?"

"There was a Board here at 10 o'clock. Were you summoned to it? If so, why do you turn up at 12.30?"

"Weel ye see, sir, I can explain that tae. I was tel't doon in the toon there that the Boord wis up here; but when I was hauf wey up a' thae duck-boords I says to masel' 'There canna be a Boord up *here!*' Sae I went awa' back to the toon again to speir if I wis richt, an' they said 'Ay'—an' a lot mair tae— an' syne I had a' the wey tae traivel back again, ye see, and that's the wey I'm late ye see, sir, for if I had keepit up thae duck-boords the first time. . . ."

"All right, that'll do! Seeing you *are* here, what's wrong with you?"

"Weel, it's just like this, sir; *I'm ower wee for the job!* When we're marchin' I'm aye fa'in ahint. Noo ye see, on the ither side o' the watter, afore I cam' oot here, there wis a sargint—Oh, an awfy fine felly, that sargint!— and when the big chaps wis stappin' out he aye says, 'Noo haud on, boys, or we'll be lossin' Wee Ginger!' (That's what they ca' me, ye see, sir.) But the sargints here's no that kind ava, an' I dinna ken hoo often they've lost me; they're aye daein't!"

He was about five feet two, and the tale sounded as if it might be lamentably true. Then I asked him—

"What did you do in civil life?"

"Weel noo, there ye are! Ye see, I wis a bird-stuffer in Glescy and that wis nae trainin' ava for *this* kin' o' a' job!"

Which was incontrovertible; so he got a fresh start in military life at the A.S.C. laundry. And I do not know whether they lost "Wee Ginger" there or not, or what sad tale of a tub he told, perchance, to the next "Boord" he encountered.

Someone has very properly remarked that the true *liaison* between the British and the French armies was the Scottish troops. The statement is curiously true—for two reasons. One is that many of the English had never got away from the "d---- foreigner" idea of the Napoleonic wars: the other, that the sentiment of the "Auld Alliance" persisted strongly amongst the French, both military and civilian. I trust that it now exists more strongly than ever and that it will last for all time.

Less, of course, the Gunners, R.E., M.G.C., A.S.C., and R.A.M.C., the 51st Division was a kilted division. I think it was Max O'Rell who gave as a reason for the Scots wearing kilts that their feet were too big to get into trousers. And we all know Joffre's classic criticism of the garb of old Gaul, so I need not—fortunately—quote it. But I once overheard in Picardy a somewhat Joffrian explanation given by an R.A.M.C. private to a French lady, of why his unit, then billeted in a village amongst kilted troops, did not also wear the *courte jupe*. The lady's knowledge of English was on par with his knowledge of French, so the conversation started by her pointing to his slacks and ejaculating "Anglais?"

"Na, na!" said he, "Ecossy!"

Whereupon she indicated a passing Jock and stated her case briefly— "Ecossais—Voila! Vous—Anglais!"

"Ach! The kilt!" he replied: "Na, na: owre muckle bendin' aboot oor job, wifie! Compree?"

I do not think she did, and perhaps as well. But the honest woman, as she set off up the road, must have gathered from the laughter of his comrades that there was some "dooble ong-tong" in the answer.

*   *   *

Now, if anyone a year before had told me that one mirk midnight, twelve months later, I should have been trudging through the mud down a back street in a picturesque and insanitary French village, my light, a three parts worn out 1 fr. 50 electric lamp, my companion an excited peasant (whose one plaintive and constant remark was "Mais depechez-vous, Monsieur!"), and my errand under the auspices of Lucina—then to that man I should have said "C'est un cauchemar!" But I depechied, all the same, and it was a fine baby, *la petite Suzanne*. (I trust she is now as well and thriving as she was when, two months subsequently, I, at the request of *maman*, kissed the infant goodbye. It was a tearful parting, and in the confusion *maman* kissed me. *Que voulez-vous? C'est l'habitude du pays!* And, *grâce à Dieu*, I dodged kissing the father, who wished to share in the compliments!)

When we passed from labour to refreshment, we broached (*sans cérémonies*, as my still excited host put it) an excellent bottle of St. Julien; and over it *la belle-mere* waxed confidential, giving the births, deaths and other medical memorabilia of her married career. She roused in time the spirit of competition in her *commère* (*kimmer* of our Franco-Scottish past) who beat her at the post, after a ding-dong race of tongues, by two infants and three dangerous illnesses. *Monsieur*, overcome with paternity—it was his first experience—nearly brought bad luck on the house by thoughtlessly lighting a third candle; and I assisted the old ladies to rub in the wickedness—especially on an occasion like this when it behoved us all to keep the auspices favourable—of trifling in this way with the popular beliefs of Picardy. He described himself, with an abandon of gesture, as being *désolé*; and I think he felt it, for he was of the large-bodied and simple-minded type. Then, after much interchange of felicitations, into the darkness and the mud again, with the big guns booming in the distance, and the occasional gleam of the star shells as "merry dancers".

The Lucina department grew and multiplied. Rumour had it that *chariots*, filled with matrons in the straw thereof, were arriving from neighbouring villages under cover of night; and this rumour we, the regular practitioners, ultimately traced to the Transport Officer, who held himself horsily aloof from general practice. But, in any case, it so happened one night that we needed an important piece of the obstetricians's armamentarium, which, *nom d'un petit bonhomme!* is not in the Mobilisation

Table, nor yet in the Field Medical Panniers! The Quartermaster, interrupted in his evening bridge, wearily suggested trying Ordnance, but curtly refused the ambassadorship. And yet it was necessary to act! Therefore in a motor ambulance wagon to the neighbouring medical unit at Esbart. Did they keep a "Simpson's long, pair, one?" *Hélas, non!* But (happy thought!) they had heard of a retired French medical practitioner who, fallen heir to a paternal *brasserie*, had shown his commonsense by abandoning medicine and brewing beer—"and very doubtful stuff at that"—in the vicinity. To him, then, post-haste at midnight to rouse him from his slumbers and recall his pre-beer days!

A long parley through shuttered windows with his good lady, ultimately ended in our admittance; although, misunderstanding our design, she insisted that under no circumstances could *monsieur* go out as he was a sufferer from *la bronchite*. Bearded, stout, asthmatic yet amiable, he at last descended, with all his kindly soul in his "Qu'y-a-t-il pour votre service?" The case is explained. A Simpson's, long, pair, one? "Mais non, monsieur?" Mieux que ça! Tarnier! Did we in our country know of this immortal?" Duly assuring him that all true Scots obstetricians grovelled at his shrine, we left with a highly rusted museumesque antique—a candidate for the steriliser.

Coelum non animum mutant! Il n'y-a rien de nouveau sous le soleil!

> Through broken nights and weary days
> Lucina! Still we hymn thy praise!

It was 2 a.m. before we—three of us, for it was team-work—sat down to the first bottle of sweet champagne, in the company of the father of *la petite Jacqueline*, the two grandfathers, the two grandmothers, some cousins and other *parents*, and the *sage-femme*. It was somewhat later still when we got to the chateau where we were billeted and wakened our totally unsympathetic brother officers to tell them the glad news about France's new inhabitant. There are some souls in whom the spirit of romance is as dead as Queen Anne.

*   *   *

The comic relief at Lille Road Post was supplied by "James", one of our Hun auxiliary loaders. His real name, I suppose, was Heinrich Schneider or something of that sort; but, as he spoke good English, he was appointed interpreter for enemy wounded, and put in charge of his whole-skinned countrymen who were assisting to carry casualties down to and up from the dressing room. He had been—so he said, and there was no reason to doubt it—for ten years before the war a waiter at the Hotel Cecil, hence the temporary name bestowed on him; and his behaviour was certainly a curious mixture of the soldier and the waiter. When spoken to he came sharply to attention (military), with a gentle bend forwards from the waist (Hotel Cecil); while his prompt "Yessir!" almost made one see the napkin over his arm. Stoutish, broadish, and—to us, his captors—affable, he magnified his office with evident relish, and treated his hoplites with true Hunnish high-handedness.

From the entrance to the dressing room I overheard my colleague, who was busy with a wounded enemy casualty at one period of the first day's work, giving James a high moral lesson, in a clear, somewhat professorial style.

"You will observe, James, that here, contrary to the custom of your countrymen in this war, we treat our wounded enemies with the same consideration extended to our own troops."

"Yessir!"

"Before the war, James, I had travelled much in your Fatherland, and had failed to detect the degeneracy—"

"Yessir!"

"—which has since, evidently, developed with such alarming rapidity."

"Yessir!"

"Cruelty, on our part, is not made a matter of military routine."

"Yessir!"

"You mean 'No sir', I think, James?"

"No sir!"

"Ah, well! The case is dressed; summon your comrades."

"Yessir! *Achtung! Zwei träger! Aufheben!*"

And away went James with his compatriots to load the case on a back-going car.

After twelve hours of it, James came to me, saluted, and remarked—

"Sir, I and my men are exhausted."

"I and my men are also exhausted, James."

"Yessir! But we had no sleep for two nights before this battle."

"Right, James, I shall believe you and relieve you."

So, in charge of a sergeant, James and Co. were sent along the trench to the Divisional Soup Kitchen to have a good feed, and were thence taken below to an old French dug-out, where various worn-out bearers of our own were resting.

Later, it was reported to me that James was missing; and although we made a perfunctory search for him, we could not find him. Two hours afterwards I was passing a small recess blanketed off from the sandbag wall of the dressing-room, in which was a stretcher and some blankets, placed there for my accommodation with kindly forethought by the staff-sergeant, should an opportunity for rest come along. Hearing a stertorous snort, I pulled back the blanket and discovered James sound asleep in my bed, evidently under the impression that his "staff job" entitled him to some precedence. The humour of it tickled me so much that I left him; but his snores gave him away to others before long, and he was "put back where he belonged".

When the time came to hand him and his comrades over to the A.P.M.'s guard, James asked to see me, and giving his salute-cum-bow said—

"Sir, I trust I have given satisfaction!"

96

"Let your mind be easy, James: you have."

"Sir, I hope we shall meet again."

"When, James?"

"After the war, sir."

"And where, James?"

"At the Hotel Cecil, sir!"

With which pious hope James solemnly saluted and vanished into the gloom of the trench.

THE SCOTTISH BONE-SETTER

The smiddy stands beside the burn
That wimples through the clachan;
I never yet gae by the door
But aye I fa' a-laughin'.

[Alexander Rodger]

There are professors and "professors"—of that there is no doubt. Some are born to blush unseen—and often imperfectly heard—in the classrooms and laboratories of a University. A larger number rise to giddy heights. I have even seen with my own eyes a professor descend from the skies, and he—although you might have thought it—was not a professor of Divinity. He landed (learned man!) on his back in a turnip-field; and when we, an enthusiastic crowd, surged across the Swedes to cheer him, he rose, in his shirtsleeves and his wrath, and cursed us in the high-pitched language of London. Cursed us for viewing his parachute descent gratis from the King's highway, instead of paying for admission to an enclosure from which we would only have seen him ascend and drift out of sight. Other professors, having assumed the title and temporarily laid aside the hod and the pick, insert an advertisement in an evening paper, and "specialise". And their skill—need it be said?—is devoted to the lower disorders of the lower orders, to the relief of those who, as the Kincardineshire ploughman euphemistically described it, are "a' wrang doon about the doon-aboots."

But if the curers of "nervous debility", "youthful errors and indiscretions", and all the rest of that happy hunting-ground for the quack, are left out of account, the next great humbug, glorified and adored by an empty-headed and open-mouthed public, is the bone-setter. He may or he may not be a professor. Our colleagues in the Potteries, recognising with skilled ease the clay feet of the idol thrust on them by a duchess, refused to worship. And yet later, when the philanthropic lady was temporarily crippled, "Atkinson" was not telegraphed for: a qualified medical man—O, feminine wisdom and inconsistency!—was enough.

The Scottish bone-setter, as a rule, leaves the high-sounding title to the Southron or the Yankee, and the smoke of the "smiddy" is a good enough background to his luminous cures. For, always a humbug, the hero of our tale is frequently a blacksmith. Why this should be so I know not. Vulcan, although notoriously unsound in one of his lower limbs, did not thereby gain a reputation amongst his fellow gods of being "skeely wi' banes"; nor did Tubal Cain, so far as we know, brazen out an unwarranted surgical reputation. Per chance it fell out, in days of yore and gore, that he who made the sword-blade was looked to for healing the hurt—an unthrashed-out and rudimentary idea of a Workmen's Compensation Act. But be that as it may, it is no uncommon thing in rural Scotland for wee Jock or Jean to go astride

Mally when the honest mare needs shoeing, and for Robin Tamson to wipe his hands on his leather apron and "put in" a fabulous number of the bairn's bones, to the admiration of his cronies.

Of knowledge of anatomy or of training our friend has none. Of this, more even than of his skill, he is proud. For is it not a matter of "heir-skep"? Did not his father before him, or at least his grandfather, or at the very worst his aunt, possess "the touch" in their day and generation? *Nascitur non fit*—"It rins in the bluid." A medical man may study anatomy and surgery for years, he may practise with success as a howdie or a pill-giver, but "a' body kens doctors ken naethin' aboot banes". And so hey! for the horny-handed hammer-holder when an injured limb cries out for real heaven-given unadulterated skill.

I suppose every country practitioner in Scotland could tell of cases ruined by these charlatans. I know of one case where, after the rough handling of a tuberculous ankle-joint (three bones were, of course, "put in", and the medical attendant's nose—equally, of course—put out), suppuration occurred in the joint, followed by general septicaemia and death. I know of another case where, after being thrown out of a trap, a man was content for a fortnight with the ministrations of a platelayer on the railway. When the patient came to me he had a fracture of the surgical neck of the humerus, with a subglenoid dislocation of the head of the bone. This was subsequently excised in hospital, and the patient, always a weakly man, died at home some months later. And so on *ad nauseam*.

All this makes for tragedy. But the prevailing note is more often that of comedy. Take the case of the little Fife boy who had been taken by his parents to see a "bone-doctor" about a "sair leg". After as much headshaking, condemnation of the medical attendant, etc., as were thought necessary, several bones were put in, and the child brought home. A kindly neighbour enquired if he had suffered much pain. "No fear!" said the wee chap, "dae ye think I was sic a saftie as gie him the sair leg?" And, again, not a hundred miles from the "Lang Toon", and not a hundred years ago either, two drouthy cronies were swaying homewards, when one said to the other— "Lie doon, Jock! here's the bane-doctor. Sham that ye've gotten a bane oot." Down with great ease sank Jock, and the "skeely" one gave his aid with such right goodwill that the practical joker was left on the pavement with a very genuine dislocation of the hip.

What (beyond "heir-skep") are their qualifications? *Nil.* A bone-setter, however, has some limit to his powers. Whatever else he can put in, he cannot put in a certificate that will satisfy an accident insurance company. Not long ago I was asked to see a ploughman who had fallen off a cart. I found him with a Colles' fracture, the injured part covered with a stinking greasy rag, above which were firmly whipped two leather bootlaces. The bones were not in position, and the hand, from interference with the circulation, was in a fair way to become gangrenous. Yet the injury had been met with a week previously, and he and his employer had been highly pleased with the treatment. I was only wanted to fill in the insurance schedule.

On another occasion I was visited by a genial ploughman who wished me to "tak' a look at his back". He, too, had fallen off a cart. When? Oh, a fortnight ago. Why hadn't he come sooner? Oh, he had been at a bone-doctor. Why did he come here now? And then came the story. "Weel, ye see, doctor, he tell't me he had pit in the bane that rins frae the middle o' the back-bane richt through to the breist-bane, and I thocht he had dune fine! But the mistress and me, the ither nicht, was lookin' up an auld medical buik wi' an atomy intilt, and we fund there wisna sic a bane there. So I thocht I'd see what *you* said aboot it!" I said a good deal about it.

A coachman, who had been flung off his box and got a bruised elbow, had thirteen small bones put in at the elbow-joint by one famous blacksmith still in practice. This same bone-setter (who has had a belted earl as his patient) stated to a man, who in turn retailed it to me, that he had been offered £600 a year by a London hospital to go there and do nothing but set bones. But what is mere money to the true philanthropist? Jingling dross! He declined the offer!

One curious qualification for bone-setting was given me by a collier who had been to a bone-setter with a "staved thoom". I asked him why he had gone there. "Lord, man! I dinna ken. They a' say he's unco skeely." But what training had he? "Weel, he was aince in a farm, and drank himsel' oot o't!" A rapid, easily passed curriculum, possessed even of a certain attractiveness for some minds.

To take a few amongst many Fifeshire bone-setters, we find the following occupations—schoolmaster, blacksmith, quarryman, platelayer, midwife, and joiner. The blacksmith, the joiner, and the platelayer are still with us; the others have crossed the Styx.

What is their *modus operandi?* Like the spelling of the historical name of Weller, it "depends upon the taste and fancy" of the individual. A rough and ready massage plays an important part, as does the implicit faith of the patient. The fearlessness of utter ignorance leads them to deal with adhesions in joints in the most thorough-going fashion, and we hear of their successes—not their failures. Many of them have the gift—a gift also common to many who never use it as hereditary skill—of making a cracking noise at the thumb or finger-joints by flexion and extension. When an injury is shown for treatment, the bone-setter handles it freely, says how many bones are "out", and then works away at the joint, making cracking noises with his own fingers, each separate noise representing one of the patient's bones returning to its proper position. "They maun hae been oot," says the sufferer afterwards, "I heard them gaun in!" Seeing may be believing, but hearing "cowes a'".

And who are their patrons? There's the rub! Not only the *profanum vulgus.* The duchess elbows the dustman at the charlatan's door, the clergyman lends his pony-trap to the collier to drive past the house of the doctor and go to the smithy. In my own district at present there is an old woman with an unreduced backward dislocation of the ankle-joint. Years ago, when injured in the harvest field, she was conscientiously carted in a clerical gig past four medical door-plates, and handed over to the ministrations of a joiner. Those of us who remember Sequah in his palmy days—palm-oily, prairie-oily: choose your own adjective—will remember how Edinburgh Waverley Market was hung round with ecclesiastical testimonials, and, doubtless, their fervent blessings have followed the ready Red Indian to wherever he may have retired. But why blame the parson when the peer gives him a lead? And why blame the peer, of all men, for a belief in hereditary gifts? If a qualification for putting out laws, why not for putting in bones?

The remedy? Legislation, of course; and, preferably, "something lingering with boiling oil in it".

THE OBSTETRIC FOLK-LORE OF FIFE

And I wish the reader also to take notice, that in writing of it I have made myself a recreation of a recreation; and that it might prove so to him, and not read dull and tediously, I have in several places mixed, not any scurrility, but some innocent, harmless mirth, of which, if thou be a severe, sour-complexioned man, then I here disallow thee to be a competent judge; for divines say, there are *offences given*, and *offences not given but taken.*—Isaac Walton.

FIFE—the home of Ptolemy's Celtic Vernicomes; "the beggar's mantle with the fringe of gold"; the potential asylum (were a wall round it) for all Scottish lunatics; the great "Kingdom"; call it what you will, and think of it how you may—has this at least in common with the rest of Scotland and the world before the Flood, that in it there is marrying and giving in marriage, and, after a more or less lengthy interval, the need for the services of the howdie. Although Kipling claims the first place of all for another nominee, the profession of the howdie is, in the nature of things, of hoary antiquity. And it is from her that we get our folk-lore in this line, although it is not always easy to find out how much is a genuine widespread folk-belief, and how much is due to the individual vivid imagination of some garrulous hag.

Nowadays we have to deal (I speak not as a guinea-coining gynaecologist, but as a weather-worn Gideon Gray), not so much with the handy-woman whose knowledge is wholly empiric, as with the widow of forty, who is expected, in a few months at a Maternity Hospital, to forget and unlearn all the dirty habits and superstitions of her class, and to become a disciple of Lister, with cleansed mind and finger-nails, and a due sense of submission to the authority of the doctor. Results, of course, are not always up to expectation: *naturam expellas furca, tamen usque recurret* [what is bred in the bone will come out in the flesh].

Of the rural Sairey Gamp, *pur sang*, I knew only one typical example. She lived in a picturesque and insanitary Perthshire village where she practised her art with no small acceptance. Her husband—strange conjunction of the cradle and the grave—was the village grave-digger, and while I was there the advancing years of Gabriel Grub and herself compelled her to drop her *clientele* and retire into private life. She kindly called me to her house, where (after carefully impressing upon me the grief the necessity caused them) she told me of several "heavy-fittit" ladies who, failing her, would now need to be content with me. Various were the valuable hints she gave me as to how to conduct their lying-in in a manner suitable to their several temperaments, and one I remember well. "There's Mrs. W., up the close there; she's expeckin' her sixth this week. I've been wi' her wi' them a', and she'll get on fine till the hinder-en'. *But there's an awfu' heuk at the fit o' her back-bane*, so ye'll hae to bide your time till it gies a crack, and syne the bairn'll come hame wi'oot ony mair fash." I duly attended Mrs. W., found she had an anchylosed coccyx which obstructed labour, waited for the prophesied "crack", and "syne there was nae mair fash". Now that howdie was not altogether an ignorant fool: she could observe, and cautiously, Cuttle-like, "when found make a note of".

History tells us that the mother of Socrates was a midwife. He showed his inclination to the paths of wisdom early in life by not taking up the profession of his mother. We (many of us at all events), without the excuse he might have urged of hereditary bias, have shown less sense, and are now subject at all hours to the excited summons of the perspiring male parent. And in the pursuit of this branch of our profession we have our little joys and sorrows; the joy of entering the house, saying (beneath our breath, of course), with Meg Merrilees—

> Canny moment, lucky fit!
> Is the lady lighter yet?

and trying decently to hide our joy when we find we are only in time to express regret—and the placenta.

And the sorrow of it when we are too soon! When we sit with our feet on the fender and read thereon the tantalising legend, in ornamental brass letters, that there is "Nae place like hame"; when we shift our tired bones about on a hard wooden chair (for the easy-chair, with its greasy, burst cushion, suggests entomology), and try to dodge the persistent draught; when we lay our head on the ingle-cheek and smoke a surreptitious pipe up the chimney; when in a low voice we talk local scandal with the "neebor" till the patient fretfully asks, "How ony ane can hae bairns wi' a' that talkin' gaun on"; when we rake up from the recesses of our sleepy memory all the appropriate and consolatory proverbs we can; when we wish either that Eve had not eaten that apple or that we had gone in for the kirk; when our eye roams wearily, in the smelling paraffin lamp-light, from the china dogs to the very German "Woman of Samaria", and back to the wooden money-box telling us in broken verse that

> John Andrew Brown Paterson is not a fool,
> He puts his pennies in his stool;

when we hear John Andrew (soon to be "put in the stirky's sta'") muttering in his disturbed sleep, or see him gazing round-eyed at the horrible spectacle of a strange man at his fireside where no strange man ought to be; when—O, Lucina! what rural obstetrician knows it not by heart, chapter, verse, and fustian binding?

Well, we are only doing what others have done before us and will after us, perhaps with more, perhaps—who knows?—with less credit, one thing alone certain, terribly under-paid for the time and nerve-wear. John Brown quotes an unknown follower of the Crambo-clink who sang feelingly in 1817 what we can equally well sing now—

> For days and nights in some lone cottage,
> Content to live on crusts and pottage,
> To kick his heels and spin his brains

> Waiting, forsooth, for labour's pains;
> And that job over happy he
> If he squeeze out a guinea fee!

For all the fathers in the land are not so fore-handed or so free-handed as the "Jollie Beggar" who

> Took the lassie in his arms
> And gae her kisses three,
> And four-and-twenty hunder merk
> To pay the nurse's fee,

nine good months and maybe a day or two before it was called for.

So much—too much, perhaps—for preface. In what follows I have to some extent drawn on a previous paper,[1] but I have thought the matter of sufficient interest to bear some elaboration. May those who read this think the same.

The commencement of menstruation is described as "comin' the length o' a woman", "turnin' no weel o' hersel'", or "seein' her ain". A woman who has missed a period will say that "her ain has left her", and when this happens finally she is said to be "past the change". In cessation of the lochia the patient is said to be "dried up" (in India the natives call puerperal fever "the dry disease"), while a woman who menstruates during lactation is said to be a "green nurse". As regards menstruation, it is steadfastly believed by the vulgar that any substances such as jam or preserves made by a menstruating woman will not keep, but will, for a certainty, go bad. Not long ago, I was told in all seriousness that a newly-killed pig had been rendered quite unfit for food through being handled by a woman "in her courses", all curing processes being useless to check the rapid decomposition that followed. Here, of course, we have traces of Mosaic law.

When a woman becomes pregnant, she is said to be "on the road", "heavy-fittit", "gettin' stout", or, more plainly but less politely, "breedin'". A husband engaging a medical man for his wife's "doon-lyin'" may delicately refer to the lady as being "in the way o' weel daein'".

There is a popular belief that when pregnancy commences the husband is frequently afflicted with toothache or some other minor ailment, and that he is liable to this complaint until the birth of the child. This can be compared with the present-day *couvade*, still in vogue among some savage tribes, where the husband goes to bed to undergo a luxurious and complimentary pseudo-puerperium, while the mother has to fend for herself as best she may.

In *Aucassin and Nicolete* (*circa* 1130), as done into English by Andrew Lang, we have an interesting reference to the *couvade* of that day. When Aucassin, in his wanderings in search of Nicolete, came to the strange land of Torelore, he asked for the king, and was told he was in child-bed, while the queen was away with the army! So

Aucassin, the courteous knight,
To the chamber went forth-right,
To the bed with linen dight,
Even where the king was laid.
There he stood by him and said,
'Fool, what mak'st thou here abed?'
Quoth the king, 'I am brought to bed
Of a fair son, and anon
When my month is over and gone,
And my healing fairly done,
To the minster will I fare,
And will do my churching there,
As my father did repair.'

But Aucassin disapproved of this practice, and not being a folk-lorist, he thrashed the king with a cudgel, remarking, "By God's head, thou ill son of an ill wench, I will slay thee if thou swear not that never shall any man in all thy land lie-in of a child henceforth for ever." "So the king did that oath," quoth the chronicler, and small blame to him under the circumstances, even though he had conscientious objections. In a note, Andrew Lang says, "The feigned lying-in of the father may have been either a recognition of paternity (as in the sham birth where Hera adopted Heracles), or may have been caused by the belief that the health of the father at the time of the child's birth affected that of the child."

So for Torelore; but in Fife some similar and subtle sympathy evidently exists between the health of husband and wife. Not so long ago a man came to me to have a troublesome molar extracted. When the operation was over he remarked, in all earnestness, "I'm feared she's bye wi' again, doctor! That tooth's been yarkin' awa' the last fourteen days, and it's aye been the way wi' me a' the time she's carryin' them." Another patient lately assured me that her husband "aye bred alang wi' her", and that it was the persistence of toothache in her unmarried adult son which led her to the (correct) suspicion that he had broken the seventh commandment, and made her a grandmother.

A confinement is referred to as a "cryin'",[2] "a cryin' match", or "howdie wark". The woman may also be said to be "in the hole", or "in the strae". If her confinement may come off at any time, she is "at the doon-lyin'". While every Cockney can tell you nowadays that a "howdie" is a midwife, fewer people know that the slang Scots term for an accoucheur is a "finger-smith".

Pregnancy is frequently dated from taking a "scunner" (disgust) at certain articles of food—tea, fish, etc. If the confinement is misdated, the woman whose calculations have gone wrong is said to "have lost her nick-stick". While the woman is pregnant she must not sit with one leg crossed over the other, as she may thereby cause a cross-birth. If she is much troubled with heart-burn, she may rest assured that her future offspring will have a good head of hair; while a dietary embracing too much oatmeal will cause trouble to those washing the child, as it produces a copious coating of *vernix caseosa.*

Many mothers believe that the tastes (likes and dislikes) of the child are dependent on the mother's diet while pregnant, *e.g.* a woman who has eaten much syrup will have a syrup-loving child.

When the child appears in the world it may have a caul ("coolie", "happie-hoo", or "hallie-hoo") over its face. This is a sign of good luck, and is still frequently preserved. I was shown one fifty years old not long ago by its owner, who, as it happens, has been a peculiarly unfortunate woman. Some hold that if given to a friend it will serve as a barometer of the donor's health. If in good health the "happie-hoo" keeps dry; if the giver turns ill the hood becomes moist. Henderson,[3] quoting the Wilkie MS., says, "Children born with a 'halli-hoo' (holy or fortunate hood) or caul around their head are deemed lucky, but the caul must be preserved carefully, for should it be lost or thrown away the child will pine away, or even die. This superstition, however, is world-wide, and of such antiquity as to be reproved by St. Chrysostom in several of his homilies. It still prevails in France, where its universality is attested by a proverbial expression—*etre né coiffé*, which means to be prosperous and fortunate in everything." Among the Boers this belief turns up also.

In an interesting article in a recent *Spectator* we find that strange properties are possessed by the *man met die helm*. "One often hears the expression, 'I am afraid of so and so; he has been born with the helm.' . . . As long as they preserve the covering (which the nurse carefully removes and dries) they are able to look into the future, and to possess a kind of second sight. A man born with the helmet foresees the death of a near relation by seeing a funeral procession pass in front of his bedside; and numerous instances are on record, it is alleged, of accurate forecastings on the part of such singularly gifted beings." Sailors believe in a dried caul as a prophylactic against drowning. Captain Marryat, amongst others, mentions this, and in France the possession of a dried caul gives eloquence to an advocate. It might be possible to establish a lucrative trade in such articles amongst would-be M.P.s.

But to return to our infant. The nurse examines the child to see that it is "wice and warl'-like", and that there are no signs of its being an "objeck" or a "natural". She may object to washing the bairn's "loof"[4] (palm) as being unlucky, and doing away with its chance of acquiring wealth; she will certainly object, on the same grounds, to your weighing the new arrival, or, later on, suggesting that its nails should be cut. If the child micturates freely at birth, it is considered a sign of luck for the child and for all who may participate in the benefit.

If the little stranger is a plump child we are told, "That ane hasna been fed on deaf nuts." Should the child have "hare-shaw" (hare-lip) or "whummle-bore" (cleft palate), there will naturally be much chagrin; but a "bramble-mark" or "rasp" (naevus), unless on the face, is not objected to, as it is supposed to indicate future wealth. Such marks are held to increase in size and darken in colour as the fruits in question ripen.

The belief in maternal impressions is, of course, fixed and certain, and wonderful are the tales told of children born with a snap on the cheek (through that favourite piece of confectionery having been playfully thrown at the mother) or with a mouse on the leg—the only wonder being that, with the prevalent female objection to mice, any child should escape having a mouse maternally impressed somewhere. Most children, as we all know well, are born "tongue-tackit" (tongue-tied), and speedy surgical interference is suggested or requested.

While labour progresses, the sex of the child—apart from all the theories of the late Schenk[5]—is discussed by the howdie. One school of specialists maintains that "a laddie is carried mair to the front, a lassie to the back"; another hold that "a lassie is carried high up, a laddie laigh doon", or tersely and metaphorically, "the laddie bides nearest the door". It is also well known as regards the male parent that "ony laddie can get a laddie; it needs a man to get a lassie", a saying that may afford a modicum of consolation to the many-daughtered. If the child's first cry can be twisted into "dey" (father), the next comer will be a male. (Henderson says that according as the child says "papa" or "mamma" first, so will the next child be male or female. This is a long time to wait, and Fife goes faster.) The "toom" cradle should not be rocked as it gives the child a "sair wame". The Wilkie MS. quotes in this connection:

> Oh! rock not the cradle when the baby's not in,
> For this by old women is counted a sin,
> It's a crime so inhuman, it may na be forgi'en,
> And they that wi' do it hae lost sight of heaven.

This belief holds also in the south of Scotland, Holland and Sweden. The child should always, where possible, be carried upstairs before it is carried down, and where this is impossible, a box or a chair will give the necessary rise in life. If the teeth come soon it leads to the prophecy, "Sune teeth, sune mair",[6] crystallising the belief that the infant will not have a long lease of his cradle before turning out for the next tenant; while

> They that get their teeth abune
> Will never wear their marriage shoon

explains itself. While discussing teeth it is worth noting that when a milk-tooth is shed it should be put in the fire with a little salt, and either of the following verses repeated:

> Fire! fire! burn bane!
> God gie me my teeth again!

or

> Burn! burn! blue tooth,
> Come again a new tooth!

In dividing and tying the umbilical cord, beware! take care! For he whose navel-string is cut too short will, when his time comes, run the risk of being a childless man. Would it not be an act of international courtesy—the Franco-Scottish Society might issue a leaflet—to let our neighbours across the Channel warn their accoucheurs? Two inches more per male child, and in a couple of generations a doubled population, and—*La revanche!*

During her puerperium the mother must take care not to "redd" her hair nor even to "reach abune her breath" until the ninth day. Nor if she take a "grewsin" (rigor) must she touch her mammae, or a "beelin' breist" will be her sure reward.

These are a few—can I safely say a select few?—of the folk-beliefs that still linger round rustic firesides what time the shortbread and whisky (degenerate remains of the "shooten" and the "groanin'-maut") are being looked forward to as the termination of weary hours of waiting—not, of course, by the patient or the doctor—but by the Rabelaisian lady-help, well steeped in the lore of the flesh and the devil. If not always instructive, they usually are, to a certain extent, amusing to those endowed with the saving sense of humour. To those who are not, I can only say with the St. Andrews' worthy—

> I shrew thame that ay leiss but lauchter,
> Quod Symmie to his bruder.

For, to quote the preacher, "A merry heart doeth good like a medicine, but a broken spirit drieth the bones"; and, when the black bag is flung into the trap on a weary winter's night, a merry heart is no small addition to our "gibbles".

1 'On Some Scots Words, Proverbs, and Beliefs, bearing on Diseased Conditions', *Transactions of the Royal Philosophical Society of Glasgow*, 1900.
2 Burns, 'O wha will tent me when I cry?'
3 *Folk-Lore of the Northern Counties of England and the Borders*, Folk-Lore Society, 1872.
4 Burns, 'The gossip keekit in his loof'.
5 [Leopold Schenk, a writer upon the determination of sex.]
6 'Soon teeth, soon toes' in Durham.

Glossary

adae ado
ae one
a'-gate everywhere
aglee amiss
ailin' sick, ill
ails, a. ye at is wrong with
airt direction, quarter
an if
apotheck lot, concern
argy-bargy quarrelsome argument
ase-puckle spark from fire
attour over
Auld Ane, A. Geordie, A. Hornie, A. Nick, A. Nickie-Ben, A. Sootie the Devil
awa, fair a. wi't gone off; in the state of death; 'done for'
awyte affirmative expression
ayont beyond
A.D.M.S. Assistant Director Medical Services

ba' ball; *to get on the b.*, to go on a jollification
bade stayed, resided
baird beard
ban curse, abuse
bane-doctorin' bone-setting
bar joke, good tale
bauchles old down-at-heel shoes
bawsent streaked white on face
bedfast confined to bed
beelin' suppurating
beerit buried
bejaupt caked
besom a worthless woman
bide to dwell; wait
bield shelter
biggin building
billy fellow
binna be not
birl move rapidly
birr energy
birse bristle; *to get your b. set up*, to be made angry
birsin' rubbing
bit, at the b. at the crisis
blade a gallant
blaw boast
blether talk nonsense

body, beast or b. lower animal or man
bogie-roll black twist tobacco
bogle apparition
bonnet-laird small landed proprietor
bourachie crowd
branks halter, bridle
brizz press
broddit gored
brods boards
brookit grimy, streaked with soot
bubbly-jock turkey
Buchan the author of 'B.'s Domestic Medicine'
bude was compelled to
buller roar
burr prickly seed-case or head of certain plants
busk to deck, adorn
but-an'-ben two-roomed cottage
buttery flattering
bye wi't done for
byornar extraordinary
byous very

ca' drive, work; *c. owre* overturn
ca' call
cahoochy indiarubber
caird tinker, tramp
caller fresh
cankert ill-natured
canny careful, cautious
carle old man, churl
chack nip
chaft cheek
chappit struck
cheeky-on in a lop-sided manner
cheep squeak, faint sound
chief friendly, intimate
chiel stripling, a term of intimacy
chimbley-cheek hearth
clachan hamlet
clanjamphry mob, riff-raff
clarty dirty
clatter noisy talk
cloot patch
clour a blow
coats, coaties petticoats
cockernony gathering of a woman's hair into a 'snood' or fillet
cod pillow

cogie a wooden vessel for holding drink, etc.
connach waste, destroy
conter thwart, contradict
coup upset
couthy pleasant, agreeable
crack gossip
craig throat
crambo-clink rough rhyme, doggerel
cramoisie crimson
cranreuch hoar-frost
creishy fat, oily
crine shrivel, grow small with age
crockanition utter destruction
cry to be in labour
cryin' accouchement
cuits ankles
curn a party, an indefinite number
cut, ken the c. know the type, style
cutty short clay pipe
C.C.S. Casualty Clearing Station

dab, dinna lat d. keep it secret
daddin' striking, hitting
dagont mild expletive
daikerin' strolling
dandrin', dannerin' strolling
dang drove
darg day's work
daw dawn
dawtie pet, term of endearment
deaf nut nut without a kernel
deave deafen
deid dead; death
deleerit delirious
deuks ducks
devaul cease, halt
dicht wipe
ding on on-fall
dinna do not
dirdum loud noise
divert amusement, entertainment
Dod mild expletive
doo pigeon; *d.'s cleckin'* two, a pigeon's hatch
dookit dove-cote
doon-bye down yonder
doon-settin' settlement in life
dootna doubt not
doup bottom
dour hard, stubborn, unyielding
dree endure
drooth thirst
drumlie turbid, muddy
duds ragged clothing
dunt blow, knock

dwam fainting turn
dwine waste away

Eck abbreviation for Alexander
efterhan' afterwards
eident industrious
eild old age; also *eld*
eildins of equal age
eith easy
elba, elbuck elbow
Elfan land of Faerie
elritch unearthly, ghostly
ense else, otherwise
ettlin' on the point of, intending
expeckin' enceinte, pregnant

fair hornie fair play
fa'n fallen
fash trouble
faurer further
favour resemble in feature
feck majority
feckless weak, incapable, worthless
Fegs corruption of 'Faith'
fell (intensive) exceedingly
ferlies wonders
figure o' fun laughable oddity
fin' feel
fire in the ee foreign body in eye
fire-en' fireplace, hearth
firin' firewood
firstlin's earliest products
fish hake triangular wooden framework on which to hang fish
flannen flannel
flee-oot on scold, abuse
fleechin' cajoling, flattering
fleg frighten
fley see *fleg*
flype turn outside in
flyte scold
fobbin' panting
forbye in addition
forcy urgent
forebears ancestors
fore-handit paid in advance
forfaughen exhausted
forrit forward; *even f.* straight on
fosh, foshen fetched
fowre, weel on f. nearly four o'clock
frait superstitious belief
freen' friend, usually meaning a blood relation; *a far-awa' f.* a distant relation
foonert foundered
fykin' trouble, effort

gaed owre   went beyond all bearing
gaffer   overseer
gait   way, street
galliard   a gallant; gay youth
gallivant   go about idly for pleasure
gang wi' the heart   agree with the inclination
gangrel   vagrant, tramp
gant   yawn
gar   make; *g. the heart rise*   sicken
gaun-aboot   wandering
gear   wealth, property; apparatus
gey   'fast', wild; very, considerably
gibbles   tools, articles, wares
gie him the name   name the child after him
gillie-callum   a Highland dance
gin   if
gird   hoop
girn   whimper, find fault fretfully
girse   grass
gizzent   warped, twisted through drought
glamourie   fascination
glaur   mud
gled   hawk
gleg   of quick perception
glist'rin'   shining
gloamin'   dusk
glower   stare, scowl
glumph   look sulky, moody
govy-dick, g. -ding   exclamation of surprise
gowpin'   throbbing
grat   wept
gravit   muffler, cravat
green   long for
greet   shed tears
grew   shiver, rigor
grewsin'   shivering
grozer buss   gooseberry-bush
groanin' maut   ale brewed to celebrate a birth
gude-mither   mother-in-law
guerdon   gift
guff   whiff, savour
gully   large knife
gurly   boisterous

haar   thick mist
hail doon   fall copiously
haill apotheck   whole concern
hairst   harvest
hame, nicht the bairn cam' h.   night the child was born
hame-wan   homewards
hantle   large quantity; much

happit   wrapped up
harns   brains
heed, tak' h.   take care
heels owre gowdie   head over heels
heicher   higher
heirskep   inheritance
herry   harass, plunder
hippen   child's napkin
hirple   hobble
hist   hasten
hives   eruption on the skin from internal cause; feverish attack
hoast   cough
holin'   digging out (coal)
hoolit   owlet
hooly   slowly
hornie, fair h.   fair exchange
horny-golloch   earwig
hotchin'   swarming
howdie   midwife
howe   hollow, small glen
howk   dig
hunker-slidin'   mean, deceitful
hurdies   buttocks
hurl   a lift on the road

ilk, ilka   each
ill-deedie   evilly disposed
ill-trickit   mischievous
in-bye   inside
ingans   onions
ingle   fireside
intil   into
intimmers   the intestines, 'inside'
I'se   I shall

jalouse   suspect, guess, imagine
jamphle   shuffle in walking
jaw   abusive talk
jimp   slender
jocoe   jocose, happy
jorum   big drink
jouk   stoop to evade a blow
joukery-pawkery   double-dealing, trickery
jucks   ducks

kebbuck   cheese
keek, keekin'-gless   peep, looking-glass
keppit   met
Kilmarnock   nightcap
kilt   tuck up
kimmer   a 'gossip'
kink-hoast   whooping-cough
kintra-side   countryside
kist   chest;   *k.o'whistles*   organ, harmonium

knee-pan knee-cap
knock clock
knowe hill, knoll

lappers clots
lasher heavy blow
lave the rest, remainder
leal-he'rtit true-hearted, loyal
lear lore
leear liar
lee-lane alone
left lateral poseetion position for giving birth when the woman lies on her side
leman illicit lover
leuch laughed
libel label
lichtsome cheerful
lift sky
lilt cheerful tune or song
limmer worthless woman
ling heather
linn precipice over which water falls
lippen to trust, have faith in
little-boukit small-sized
littlens small children
lodomy laudanum
loof palm of hand
loot stoop
loup leap
lowe flame
lowse loose; to cease work
Lucina goddess of childbirth
lugs ears
lum hat silk hat, top hat

makar maker; a poet
malison a curse
mawkin hare
mell mallet, large wooden hammer
merchant country shopkeeper
midden-heid top of dunghill
mim-mou'd affectedly proper, prudish
miracklous very drunk
mirk dark, night
mischanter mishap, accident
mischeef severe hurt, harm
mizzle-shinn'd having legs discoloured by constantly sitting in front of the fire
mools the earth of a grave
moose-wabs cobwebs
mows a joke, jest
mudge movement
mutchkin pint

M'Burney's p'int point of incision for the appendix

nabal a mean, greedy churl
narra i' the swalla narrow-throated
neb nose
neeps turnips
nice particular
nieves fists
nirled, nirlt shrunken, shrivelled
noos an'ance now and then
nosey-wax easily cheated simpleton
nott needed
no-weel unwell

O.C. Officer Commanding
or ere
orra of no account, disreputable
os opening of the cervix
owre over
oxter armpit

paidle wade
pains rheumatism
palmer to wander
pang-fu' crammed full
pawky shrewd, sly
pearlins thread-lace
pech pant, breathe hard
pen-gun pop-gun
pike pick
plain-stanes pavement
plantin' plantation
pooch pocket
pree taste
preen to deck oneself; also prink
puckle small quantity
puddens intestines
puirtith poverty
put in the stirky's sta' supplanted

quate quiet
quean damsel

rackit strained
raird clamour, a noisy tongue
ravelt confused, tangled
rax reach
reddin' straik blow got by one trying to stop a fight
redd-up put in order
reid red; reid-wud stark mad
reist to stop, arrest
rife widespread
riggin' ridge of a roof
rispin' making a harsh sound
rive tear

roup sale
routh abundance
rovin' wandering
row wrap, roll
rowt bellow
royt wild, mischievous
rudas bold, masculine
rug pull, haul, drag
runt withered old man or woman

saftness weakness of character
sair serve, satisfy; sore, sorely
sark shirt
Sassenach Southron
saugh willow
saunt saint
saut salt
scart scratch
scoug take shelter from
screich, screigh shriek; *S. of day* day-
  break
scunner disgust
Seelie fairy
set kind, manner, type
sets suits
shakers nervous tremors
shauchle shuffle in walking
shilpit weak, sickly
shool spade
shoon shoes
shot distorted
sib related to
sic such
siccar sure
siller wealth
silly physically weak
sinon sinew
sizzon season
skail empty
skaith injury, damage
skeely skilful
skelp smack
skirl shriek
skirly-nackit noisy half-clad child
sklim climb
skreek shriek
sleekit sly, hypocritical
slocken quench thirst
sma'-boukit small sized
smeddum mettle, spirit
smiddy smithy
smirr drizzle
smoor smother
snab upstart, apprentice
sookers for bairns 'comforters'
soondin' auscultation
sorn to sponge on

sotter bubble, sputter as in cooking
sough sigh, sound of wind
spails splinters, chips
spate flood
spitterin' hissing
spunk spirit, pluck
spunkie mischievous sprites
spunks matches
stappit stuck, placed
starns stars
staw'd surfeited
steer commotion
stiddy anvil; steady
stoiter stumble
stound ache, throb
stour dust
strae straw; *in the s.,* in labour
stramp tramp
stroup spout
styme glimpse, faint gleam
sutten-doon chronic
swat sweated
sweer reluctant
swite sweat
Symie the Devil
Sympsone, Jamie Sir James Young
  Simpson (1811–70); distinguished
  Victorian physician and obstetrician;
  introduced new long variety of ob-
  stetric forceps
syne ago, since; then, afterwards
sype ooze, soak through

tack lease
taed toad, a term of endearment
tapsalteerie head over heels
tastin' small quantity of drink
tatties potatoes
tel't told
tent care, heed
teuch tough
thae these, those
thee thigh
thig beg, entice
thocht worry, care
thole endure, bear
thonder yonder
thowless spiritless, lacking energy
thrang busy
throw through
tick credit, trust
till, till't to, to it
timmer timber, wood
tinkler tinker
tint lost
tirravee commotion

tocher dowry
tousy unkempt
tow rope
trachelt overworked
trail walk slowly
traivel walk
tramp tread
trephine trepan
trimmle tremble
troke, trokes work in a small way; odd jobs
tryst appointment
tuilzie fight
twa-fauld bent double from age or exhaustion
twal twelve
twalmont twelve months
tyne lose

ugsome disgusting, horrible
unchancy unlucky; mischievous
unco uncommon, strange
unction, unctioneer sell by auction; auctioneer
unmensefu' unmannerly
up-bye up the way
uptak intelligence

wacht big drink
wad wager
waddin' wedding
waesome woeful
wag-at-the-wa' wall-clock with pendulum and weights exposed
wale choose

wame belly
wan won; pale, dim, gloomy
wap a smart stroke
warlock wizard
warsle wrestle
wat wetted; *w. his whustle* took a drink
waur worse
wean young child
weel-a-wat affirmative exclamation
weel on intoxicated
weet wet
weird fate
werrucks corns, bunions, excrescences on feet
wersh tasteless
whiles occasionally, sometimes
whilk which
widdy gallows
winnock small window
winsome comely
wirral small, rickety child
wit sense
wricht carpenter
wrocht worked
wud mad; *reid w.* stark mad
wyte blame

yark jerk, wrench
yatter to speak incessantly and loudly
yerl earl
yetts gates
yird; yird-fast earth; earth-fast
yoke to begin, to set to with vigour
yooky itchy
yowe ewe

Index of First Lines